Detroit Free Press

time frames

Our lives in 2001 ¶ Our city at 300 ¶ Our legacy in pictures

PHOTOGRAPHY BY THE DETROIT FREE PRESS

EDITED BY NANCY ANDREWS, PETER GAVRILOVICH & MAURICIO GUTIERREZ

1942-2002

For his teaching, his
wisdom and his friendship,
we dedicate "Time Frames"
to Robert G. McGruder, the
beloved executive editor of
the Detroit Free Press.

Detroit Free Press

TIME FRAMES STAFF

EDITOR
Nancy Andrews

WRITER
Peter Gavrilovich

DESIGNER
Mauricio Gutierrez

PHOTOGRAPHY EDITORS
Todd Cross, Andrew Johnston, Craig Porter, Mary Schroeder, Pat West, Diane Weiss

PHOTOGRAPHERS
William Archie, Patricia Beck, Kirthmon F. Dozier, John Collier, David P. Gilkey, Julian H. Gonzalez, Hugh Grannum, Jennfier Hack, Ed Haun, J. Kyle Keener, Richard Lee, Kent Phillips, Eric Seals, Chip Somodevilla, Gabriel B. Tait, Susan Tusa, Paul Gonzalez Videla, Mandi Wright

LAB TECHNICIANS AND SUPPORT STAFF
Gina Brintley, Naheed Choudhry, Rose Ann McKean, Jessica Trevino, Kathryn Trudeau

COPY EDITORS
Azlan Ibrahim, Karen Joseph, Sherita Wyche Bryant

CONSULTING EDITORS
Alexander B. Cruden, Steve Dorsey, Dave Robinson

SYSTEMS EDITOR
Stephen Mounteer

SPECIAL THANKS
Ken Elenich, Richard Simon, Charles Whitman, Sue Wilson, of the Detroit Newspaper Agency

Sarah Tse of First Global Graphics

Detroit Free Press
600 W. Fort St.
Detroit, Mich. 48226
www.freep.com

OTHER RECENT BOOKS BY THE FREE PRESS:

The Detroit Almanac

Ernie Harwell: Stories From My Life in Baseball

HeartSmart Kids Cookbook

State of Glory

Corner to Copa

The Corner

Century of Champions

PC@Home

Yaklennium

Believe!

Stanleytown

To order any of these titles, please call 800-245-5082 or go to www.freep.com/bookstore

To subscribe to the Free Press, call 800-395-3300.

To order a photo or page reprint from the Free Press, call 800-245-5082.

LIBRARY OF CONGRESS CATALOGING-IN-PUBLICATION DATA

Time frames : Our lives in 2001, Our city at 300, Our legacy in pictures / Nancy Andrews, editor ; Peter Gavrilovich, text editor ; Mauricio Gutierrez, designer ; photography by the Detroit Free Press.

  p.   cm.
ISBN 0-937247-38-3
1. Detroit (Mich.) – History-Pictorial works. 2. Detroit (Mich.) – Social life and customs-Pictorial works. I. Andrews, Nancy, 1963-
II. Gavrilovich, Peter, 1949-   III. Gutierrez, Mauricio, 1971-
IV. Detroit Free Press.
F574.D443 .T46 2002
977.4'34 – dc21
        2002006181

DETROIT 300
Partner Program member

Time Frames
Our lives in 2001, Our city at 300, Our legacy in pictures.
isbn 0-937247-38-3
$39.95

SPRAWL'S SQUEAL

Land invited us. We were growing beyond what urban planners saw as this metropolis only 50 years before. But that growth we now called sprawl, as if community hands gave a hearty snap to a regional tablecloth and let it spread over Oakland County's hills, Macomb and Monroe counties' plains and the farms and forests of Livingston and Washtenaw counties. Sprawl concerned us because the growth gobbled land once productive for trees and crops. And in its wake, we were leaving an old city and old suburbs built on models of community closeness. Detroit, however, was showing remarkable growth in new homes in 2001. Still, farmers like John Spezia, 61, photographed while holding an 8-day-old piglet on his farm in Leonard, were a novelty — their land now of value more for subdivisions, shopping malls and business buildings than for crops or livestock. **RICHARD LEE**

SPLITTING THE STRAIT *(next page)*

The flag snapped to a wind driven by the mail boat J.W. Westcott on a May day near the Ambassador Bridge. We were in an era of clean water on the Detroit River after decades when pollutants were carelessly dumped. But the water levels were lower in 2001 after several winters of little snow. Many wondered whether global warming was to blame. Others said it was a cycle, and that soon more water would rush between Windsor and Detroit and down the 31-mile gullet to Lake Erie. The Westcott was mysteriously swamped by the river in October. It sank, killing two crew members. The boat was recovered. **DAVID P. GILKEY**

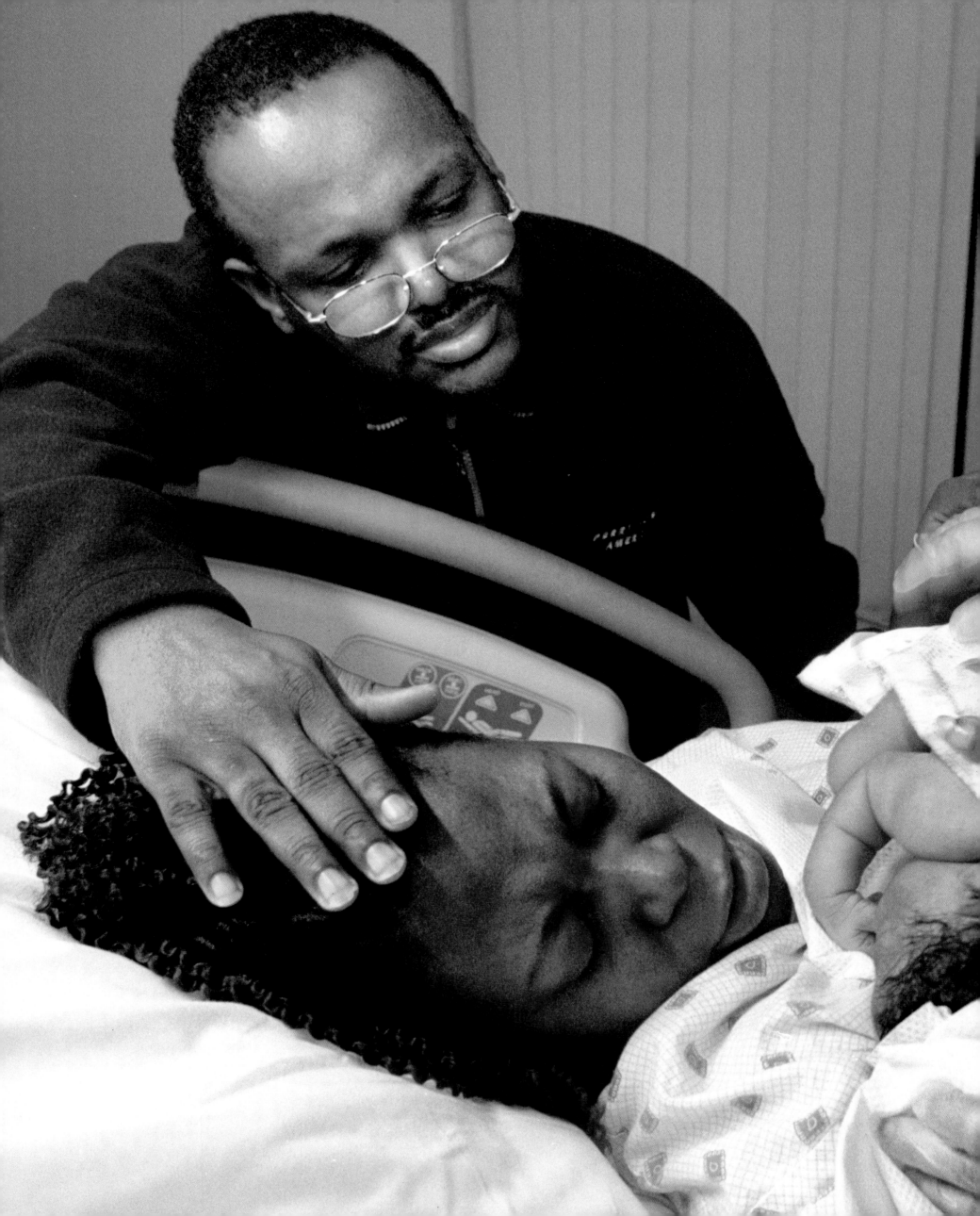

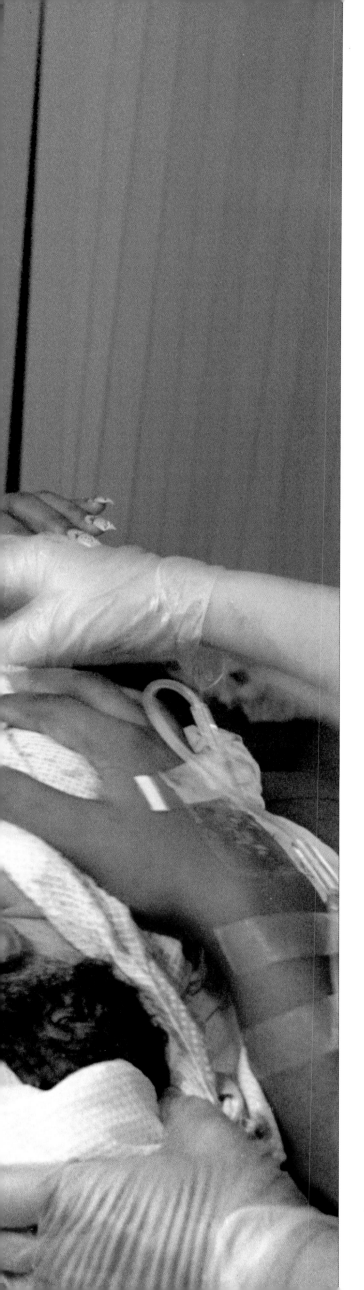

G

ENERATIONS of tomorrow inherit a memory of us as community today.

That is a legacy we pass along to our grandchildren and their children through letters and cards, an award, a dish, a doily — and pictures. Scads of pictures:

How we worked, played, dressed, traveled, shopped, worshiped, loved, obeyed, learned, lounged, led, followed, feared, ate, dated, sang, shook hands, said our prayers, waved good-bye, hugged hello.

Here is our visual time capsule. Scads of pictures. They represent our great community in 2001, when Detroit turned 300.

Each picture captures a piece of our lives, our looks, our surroundings. Some things seen on these pages will be long gone in 2051 or 2101. Certainly most of the people will be memories.

A BUNDLE OF OUR FUTURE

Birth mesmerized us. It was no less dramatic and emotional, despite the comforts and procedures of 21st-Century medicine. Beyond birth, we talked of research on embryos, and some claimed they were about to clone humans. We regularly examined wombs for gender, and for ailments, too. We expected that soon genetics would leap so far that our babies might never again grow with maladies that haunted our parents. Valicia and Larry Ward of Hamtramck — she was 27, he was 37 — celebrated the birth of their third child and first daughter at Henry Ford Hospital on Nov. 30. Her name: Anjanique Monay Ward. At her beginning, she was 7 pounds, 5 ounces. Her statistical promise was a life of 75 years. Had she been white, her life expectancy would have been about 80. Narrowing the disparity was a challenge that medical, social and government experts were trying to meet. **ERIC SEALS**

Detroiters' descendants who someday turn these pages will wonder about these days as much as people in these images wondered about tomorrow.

Will we line up at a drive-through to order a No. 5 meal? Will our sports teams have the same names or be something completely different? Will people get dressed up? Build cars? Catch fish? Donate? Embrace?

Might some kid in 2065 wonder why some kid in 2001 pushed a contraption to cut a lawn?

2001. The year would become a time capsule for countless families because of the emphasis placed on Detroit's tricentennial. This book sought to capture that emphasis from January's dressy auto show to a spring trip to a junkyard to a summer concert . . .

To 9/11. That's when the city's 300th anniversary — like so many other events across the nation — gave way to the attack that changed normal, making 2001 a monumental year for nearly everyone in the country.

In 2001, logging more than 5,000 assignments, Free Press photographers produced some 700,000 images. A newspaper photographer does more than take a picture. Photojournalists research subjects and situations, looking for the picture that will give clarity to the story, perhaps a signal of the future or a bow to the past. An action, a moment, a circumstance, a smile — all fleeting, all memories that photographers capture as chroniclers of instant history.

The instant of that history is often measured at 1/125th of a second, which means the photographs in this book as a measure of time represent 2 seconds of 2001.

Photographers write with light. For years photographers have focused light onto the silver crystals of film. Now photographers also use digital cameras with computer chips that record light in encoded pixels.

About 12 percent of the 237 images in "Time Frames" were produced with digital cameras.

We hope this pictorial cavalcade will live with your family for generations, an album of Detroit that can stand next to your personal photographs so that someday, in say 70 years, when an inquisitive child wonders what life was like way back in '01, "Time Frames" will show the answer.

ERIC SEALS

A YEAR FOR THE AGES

We watched our country come under attack on live television, stunned at the catastrophic sight of the two huge towers of the World Trade Center collapsing before our eyes, fearing for the lives of thousands we knew were in harm's way in lower Manhattan. Shoppers, above, watched the disaster unfold at a Sears store at Fairlane Mall. The year that we hoped to remember as our tricentennial became defined by the attack that plunged us into a war on terrorism. At right, as 2001 ended, Detroit Historical Museum director Dennis Zembala added an item to one of two special time capsules of 2001-era artifacts to be stored at the museum until 2101. An official Detroit time capsule containing 50 video recordings and more than 100 letters from area leaders was also sealed and placed in a vault at the Coleman A. Young Municipal Center.

PAUL GONZALEZ VIDELA

ARTWORK PACKED A PUNCH

The 8,000-pound fist of bronze and painted steel where Woodward meets Jefferson has been revered and reviled since it was bestowed upon the city in 1986 as a tribute to Joe Louis, the Detroiter who became heavyweight boxing champion. Loved because the work by California artist Robert Graham symbolizes the power of human potential. Hated because it symbolizes violence. The fist and forearm sculpture measured 24 feet long and was suspended from a pyramid 24 feet high. It was a $350,000 gift from weekly magazine Sports Illustrated. Renaissance Center, looming at right, had recently received the GM sign as the world headquarters for General Motors in this November picture. **SUSAN TUSA**

HOPE SPRANG OF STONE AND STEEL

Detroiters watched a gradual transformation at Campus Martius as high-tech company Compuware Corp. continued construction of its 15-story, 1-million-square-foot world headquarters, at right. Two years earlier, Detroit native Peter Karmanos Jr., the chairman and chief executive officer who cofounded the computer software and services giant in 1973, had announced the $350-million plan, which was to bring 3,500 high-tech professionals into the city upon the building's completion in late 2002. You're looking up Woodward; at left, the Kennedy Square project that was to include underground parking and an office building. Both projects were part of the Campus Martius plan, conceived by Detroit Mayor Dennis Archer as a development of office buildings, stores, restaurants and a hotel near Michigan and Woodward avenues. SUSAN TUSA

FIELDS OF DREAMS

Mack Avenue and Chene, on the city's near east side, on an winter day. It had been decades since this area was covered with homes and businesses. The few dwellings that remained in this section of Detroit spoke of so many areas of poverty and pain older American cities grappled with as a new century was beginning. In 2001, Detroit was tearing down housing at a clip that led the country, but the city's vacant-housing rate kept climbing. The U.S. Census Bureau reported in Detroit's 300th year that the city had a 10.3 percent housing vacancy rate when data was collected in 2000, the fourth highest in the nation. But while Detroit had a deteriorating stock of housing built during the boom times of the 1910s, '20s and '40s, something remarkable was happening here in the late 1990s and the early 21st Century: Houses were being built, too. And while numerous older sections of the city looked like Mack and Chene, there was a sense among Detroiters that maybe the worst was behind us. **NANCY ANDREWS**

CONTENTED LIFE IN THE BURBS

Through the years, many Detroiters left the city and headed for the expanse and amenities of the suburbs. Developers built spacious homes on generous plots of freshly lain, deeply green sod. A career move brought Tom and Francoise Pate from Sarasota, Fla., to an immaculate subdivision in Sterling Heights. That's Samuel Sorce, a Pate relative, standing by a buddha statue after Thanksgiving dinner at the Pate house. By 2001, the Pates had lived in their comfortable suburban nest for five years. "It's a quiet town, good shopping, all the highways are close by," remarked Francoise Pate. Sterling Heights, with a population of 125,000, was Michigan's 6th largest city in 2001. **SUSAN TUSA**

INDUSTRIAL UNDERTAKINGS

Rouge Steel Co. stood in its own grit in Dearborn on the banks of the Rouge River. On a December afternoon, marble-sized iron ore pellets were unloaded from the freighter Herbert C. Jackson. The boat had hauled the cargo from one of the Cleveland-Cliffs iron mines in the Upper Peninsula. The steel company employed 2,700 workers at the factory 10 miles west of downtown Detroit. Rouge Steel was an emblem of Detroit's automotive history, founded as a division of the Ford Motor Co. Its first steel was produced in 1923. But Ford sold the plant in 1989 to Marico Acquisition Corp.; it had operated on an independent basis since. In 2001, the plant was operated 24 hours a day, seven days a week, making flat-rolled carbon steel for the auto industry. It was surviving in an age when surviving wasn't easy. The industry had been under intense financial pressure largely because steel from Brazil, Japan, South Korea, Russia and elsewhere had flooded the domestic markets. In North America, dozens of steel mills had filed for bankruptcy since the late 1980s. SUSAN TUSA

THE UBIQUITOUS STRIP MALL

In our suburbs, the strip mall was our frequented, fragmented village square, housing grocers, eateries, hardware stores, druggists and countless other everyday necessities. And many housed our beloved video rental stores. As a nation, we were captivated by movies. We spent $8.35 billion at the box office in 2001 and $16.9 billion to buy or rent digital video discs and videocassettes. We flocked to local stores like Hollywood Video on Big Beaver near John R in Troy and plunked down $2 to $4 to take a rented video home for a night or a few days. In 2001, the stores were experiencing a crisis of space. Gradually, consumers were abandoning their videocassette recorders in favor of the more sophisticated DVD players. At the beginning of the year, 14.5 million U.S. households had DVD players, while 93 million had VCRs. For the stores, that meant carrying newly released and classic films in two formats. SUSAN TUSA

A SATURDAY MORNING RITUAL

Metro Detroiters, about 15,000 of them, converged at Eastern Market just north of Gratiot and Russell in Detroit on Saturday mornings for a ritual that predated their grandparents. More than 100 vendors and 325 farmers arrived as early as 1 a.m. to set up stalls by 7 a.m. to sell their fruits, vegetables, honey, preserves, eggs, meats, plants, flowers. The city has run markets since 1802; an earlier venue was inside city hall when that building stood in Cadillac Square. The market moved to its current location — a former cemetery — in 1887. It was the largest open-air wholesale-retail market of its kind in the United States. Regular shoppers made sure to bring a wagon or cart to haul away finds. And cash. Credit cards weren't accepted. Frugal shoppers arrived around noon, when weary farmers not wanting to load up their trucks sold produce for pocket change. **NANCY ANDREWS**

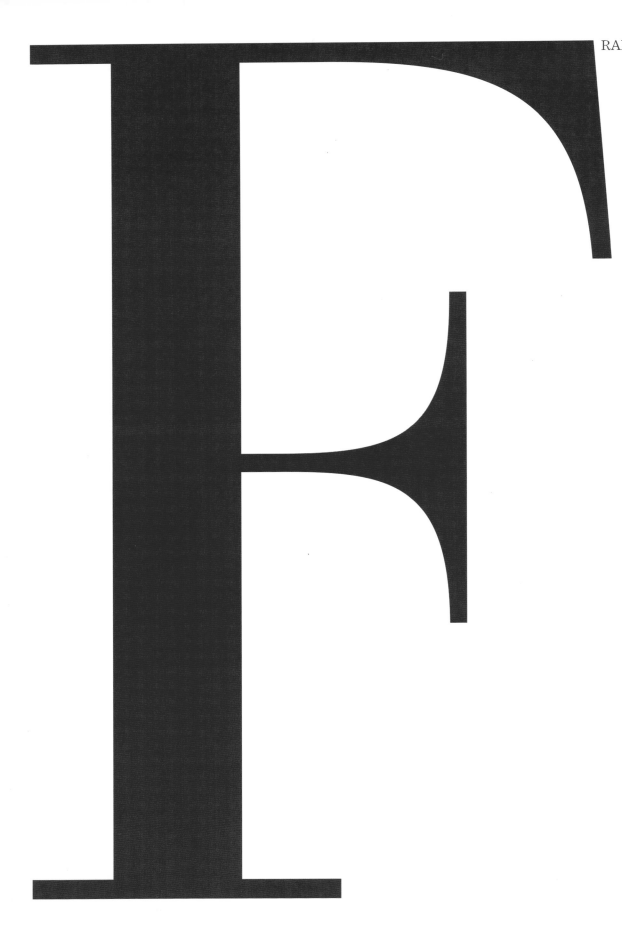

RANCE'S Antoine de la Mothe Cadillac founded Detroit with 50 men of native nations at his side, probably the best foretelling of what we have become: a city and region of so many from Africa, Europe, Asia and the Americas, of nearly all faiths of God, of diverse wills and styles of living.

The following portraits were captured by Free Press Chief Photographer J. Kyle Keener at one of Detroit's favorite places and stalwart witness to the region's diversity: the Eastern Market.

If you had gone there on Saturday, you would have found east side and west side Detroit, Taylor and Trenton, Ferndale, Farmington, Eastpointe and Westland — all Detroit's regular people, the mainstays who a day at a time helped build what we in 2001 celebrated: a 300-year-old great American city.

We were the cops, the carpenters, the chief executives and engineers, schoolteachers and pipe fitters, chefs and surgeons, dreamers and doers.

We were Muslim, Christian, Jewish and Hindu, Buddhist and Baha'i, agnostic and more; the Greeks, Poles, Senegalese, Koreans, Indians, Mexicans ... the many who added American to their heritage and proudly called themselves Detroiters whether they lived downtown or Downriver.

What started as a fur-trading settlement of a few dozen men in 1701 had become by 2001 a region of 5.3 million people. Detroit itself, however, fell to 951,000 people after phenomenal growth during the first half of the 20th Century aided by a huge migration of Southern blacks and thousands of immigrants from eastern and southern Europe. In 1955, the U.S. census estimated the city's population at 2 million; the regional population then was not even twice that number.

We became an even more diverse community by 2001, mostly because the U.S. restrictions on immigration from Asia were dropped after 1965.

Metropolitan Detroit boasted the nation's largest Chaldean-American population with more than 50,000 members, and an Arab-American population of at least 200,000.

In 2001, a year that marked a new destiny for the United States and 300 years for Detroit, we had some pretty diverse hopes and dreams, too.

WU DING, 33, a systems analyst, and her husband, Song Xu, 33, in technical sales, lived in Newport. Their hopes and dreams included "a big house and lots of kids."

1. ROBERT MEERSSEMAN, 42, Collette Meersseman, 37, and their son, Michael, 13 months, worked a family farm in Leamington, Ontario. They hoped "to live a happy and prosperous life and pass it on to future generations."

2. RUSHNA RAHMAN, 35, was a homemaker. Her brother, Monay Rahman, 55, was an autoworker, and her daughter, Shamme Rahman, 17, was a student. In front was Shamme's brother, Shahidur Rahman, 6. They lived in Hamtramck. Shamme Rahman hoped "to become successful in the medical field and help others."

TONY LIGGETT, 43, right, went by the nickname Top Kat. He lived in Hamtramck and worked as a disc jockey. He hoped "to enjoy all this city has to offer — good music, great food, excellent art — and to meet all the interesting people out there . . . Rock on!"

1. IBRAHIM TUFFAHA, 40, surrounded by his family, wife, Hana, 35, left; Mohamed, 11; Islam, 4 (on his shoulders); Ayah, 8 (in front); Alaa, 10, and Ameer, 17 months. Hana Tuffaha was a homemaker, and Ibrahim Tuffaha was a Web programmer. They lived in Dearborn and hoped for "living in peace and in good health."

2. ESTHER SHAPIRO, 83, of Detroit, a consultant and former executive for the city, wished for "health, peace and a good economy."

3. FAVIOLA CRUZ, left, 41, a janitor, and her niece, Patricia Villegas, 18, lived in Detroit. Cruz said she hoped "to send my children to college to get a better education, a better job, and to have a better life."

WALTER R. WILLIAMS, 49, right, was homeless in Detroit. He sang and played guitar and flute. He said that he hoped to be "a musician, art therapist and drama therapist."

1. STEPHANIE CHETCUTI, 23, from Detroit held two jobs. She worked with autistic children and as a barkeep. Her dream was "to start my own school. And be happy."

2. ZDZISLAW (JOHN) TOBOLA, 78, of Detroit has worked as a tool and die maker and master watchmaker. He went by John because few could pronounce Zdzislaw. His dream: "to make the people happy and healthy."

Right: DARIUS HILL, 14, and Dajuan Hill, 9, and their mother, Mattie Fleming, 42, a nursing assistant from Detroit. Fleming said she hoped she and her sons could "be the best we can be for everyone, and help the needy."

A CITY OF GENERATIONS *(previous page)*

Airplane buffs would pay $400 for a 45-minute flight in this B17 — the famed Flying Fortress of World War II. It was one of only 13 still flying in 2001 and was owned by the Yankee Air Museum/Yankee Air Force in Belleville. Here it cruised about half a mile above the city's near east side in late August. Much of the view — the subdivisions and the apartment buildings east of downtown — date to the early 1960s and later. That bright white building in Windsor was a casino. **KENT PHILLIPS**

OUR SYMBOLS OF ENDURANCE

A pickup game of basketball on a mid-summer's evening, on an asphalt court — three-on-three. There were hundreds of these contests nightly, on courts like this near Russell and East Canfield in Detroit, and in gyms and backyard courts and driveways and side streets with makeshift hoops tacked to trees or utility poles. This court was part of a neighborhood of thousands of small frame homes 100 years before this picture was taken, when those two tall spires of Sweetest Heart of Mary Catholic Church were the focus of the community. It was, in 2001, still the largest Catholic church building in Detroit, seating 2,500. But barely 60 worshipers attended the occasional Sunday services. There were few Catholics in the city proper, which was heavily Protestant.

J. KYLE KEENER

JENNIFER HACK

THEY WORKED THE LAND

Dennis Fogler was holding onto the last family-owned farm in Oakland Township in 2001 — a 1,500-acre spread. Other farms had been sold off as suburban development consumed acre upon acre of land. Fogler, 52, was unloading late-August corn at Fogler's Orchard and Farm Market. Dennis, his brother, Mike, and mother Ruth owned the business. At Eschenburg Farms in Almont, James Eschenburg, 11, helped with chores. He began driving agricultural vehicles at the corn and dairy farm when he was 8.

RICHARD LEE

PORTRAIT OF COURAGE

She had lived in Detroit for nearly half her life. Rosa Parks, in this portrait, was 88, easily the most beloved person in Detroit. When this picture was taken Dec. 1, she was surrounded by admirers at Henry Ford Museum in Dearborn. A bus, believed to be the one she boarded on Dec. 1, 1955, was being exhibited as the museum's most recent acquisition. On that 1955 day in Montgomery, Ala., Rosa Parks was ordered by the bus driver to give her seat to a white passenger. She refused. The refusal led to her arrest for violating segregationist laws, and the incident sparked the modern civil rights movement. The museum bought the rusted, gutted bus for $492,000. By 2003, the bus was to be restored and placed on permanent display. **PATRICIA BECK**

GETTING READY TO CRUISE

With the annual Woodward Dream Cruise rapidly approaching, Lynn Anderson of Clinton Township, at left, and her 11-year-old daughter Laura and 12-year-old son Paul polished the family's 1971 Volkswagen. The cruise began in 1994 and soon could claim to be the world's largest one-day car event. It catered to the culture of the car buff. More than a million people packed legendary Woodward Avenue from Ferndale to Pontiac to drive, park and gawk. The Andersons, in their Microbus Sportsmobile, were among them. **DAVID P. GILKEY**

MOWING THE BYGONE WAY

In an age when noisy, gas-powered lawn mowers were the norm, and thousands of busy home owners opted for lawn services, the old-fashioned reel lawn mowers were a rare sight. Sherriha Bragg, 9, of Detroit walked behind a push mower borrowed from a neighbor to cut the grass at her family's new house in northwest Detroit in early May. Her sister, Ashley Cooper, 3, swept trimmings from the driveway. The family lived on Lahser near 8 Mile. **GABRIEL B. TAIT**

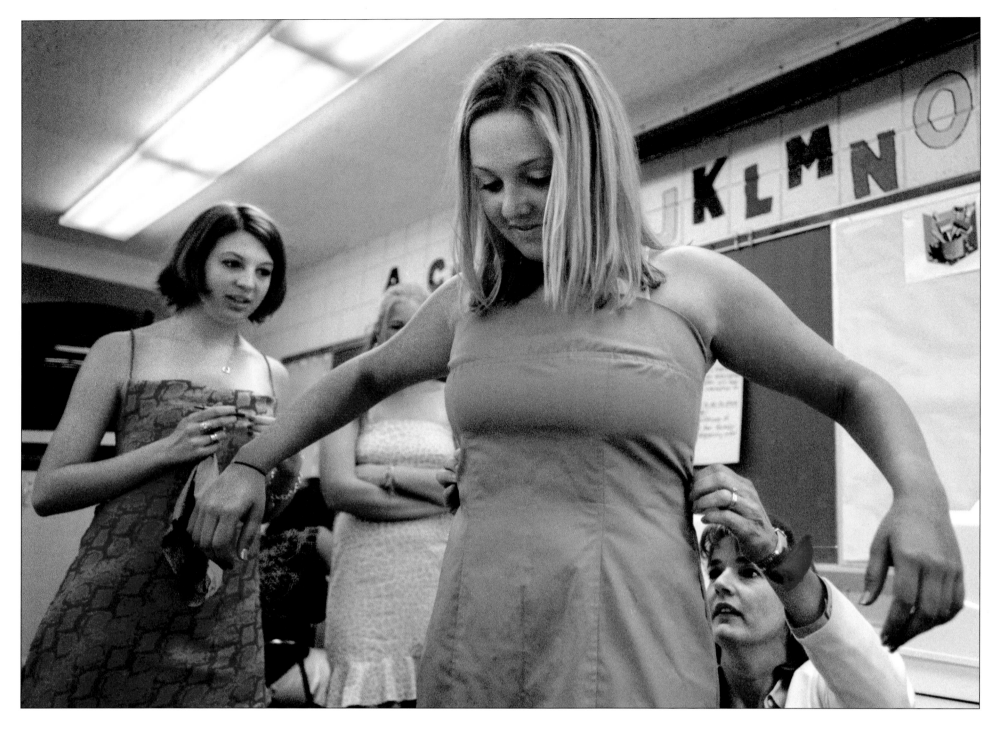

MATERIAL GIRLS

Teen interests are capricious. High school students used to learn to sew; then they didn't. Then, once again, they did. At Grosse Pointe North in May, Jamie Keller, 17, was fitted for her blue sundress. Teacher Kathy Trupiano adjusted the pins. For a dozen years in several suburbs, students weren't offered sewing classes, reflecting "a stigma attached to making your own clothes," said Linda Lethemon, a sewing and life skills teacher at North Farmington. By 2001, schools making sewing an elective had students swarming to sign up. Some schools never felt that stigma. Charity Caldwell began teaching sewing at Denby in Detroit in 1979. By 2001, her students included several boys, a gender not represented in most suburban sewing courses. **J. KYLE KEENER**

MATERIAL NEEDS

Hamtramck emerged as one of the most distinctive small towns in the country because of its amazingly diverse population. Formerly known as an automotive factory town, it had become a magnet for young people anxious to mingle among cultures. Hamtramck was a gateway community, an affordable place to live with streets still dressed with frame flats built in decades past. Storefronts turned blocks into continents' cultures. Bangladeshi natives Shazna Miah and her brother, Rashid, worked in the family's Rima Sari Center, a store that specialized in Bangali, Indian and Pakistani clothing. There were Yemeni, Bosnian, Albanian, Korean, Somali, Macedonian and Polish shops among others in the city of 23,000. **DAVID P. GILKEY**

CROSSING OVER, CAREFULLY

Linda Hammoud and 10-year-old Daniel Hubal met on the corner of Warren and Payne in Dearborn every day after school. She watched out for him the way a parent would, making sure he crossed the street only when it was safe. Daniel went to school with her daughters at Maple Elementary, where Hammoud volunteered in the cafeteria daily. By 2001, Dearborn was rapidly becoming America's most famous Arab-American city with about 33,000 Arab Americans among nearly 100,000 people. Nearly 3 of 5 students in Dearborn public schools were Arab American.
SUSAN TUSA

FIRST-DAY JITTERS

Kyla Thomas, 4, looked to her father, Ken Thomas, 29, for advice during her first day of kindergarten at Stellwagen Elementary School in Detroit. "I thought today would be easy, seeing Kyla off to her first day of school," dad recalled. "But it turns out that I'm the emotional one." Kyla likely didn't realize that her school was one of four new Detroit public school buildings that opened in 2001. Many of the district's 300-plus buildings were old, crumbling and poorly maintained. The district spent $400 million on projects to upgrade schools, including support systems for 21st Century technology. In 2001, the district had 162,000 students, more than 10,000 of them kindergartners. **GABRIEL B. TAIT**

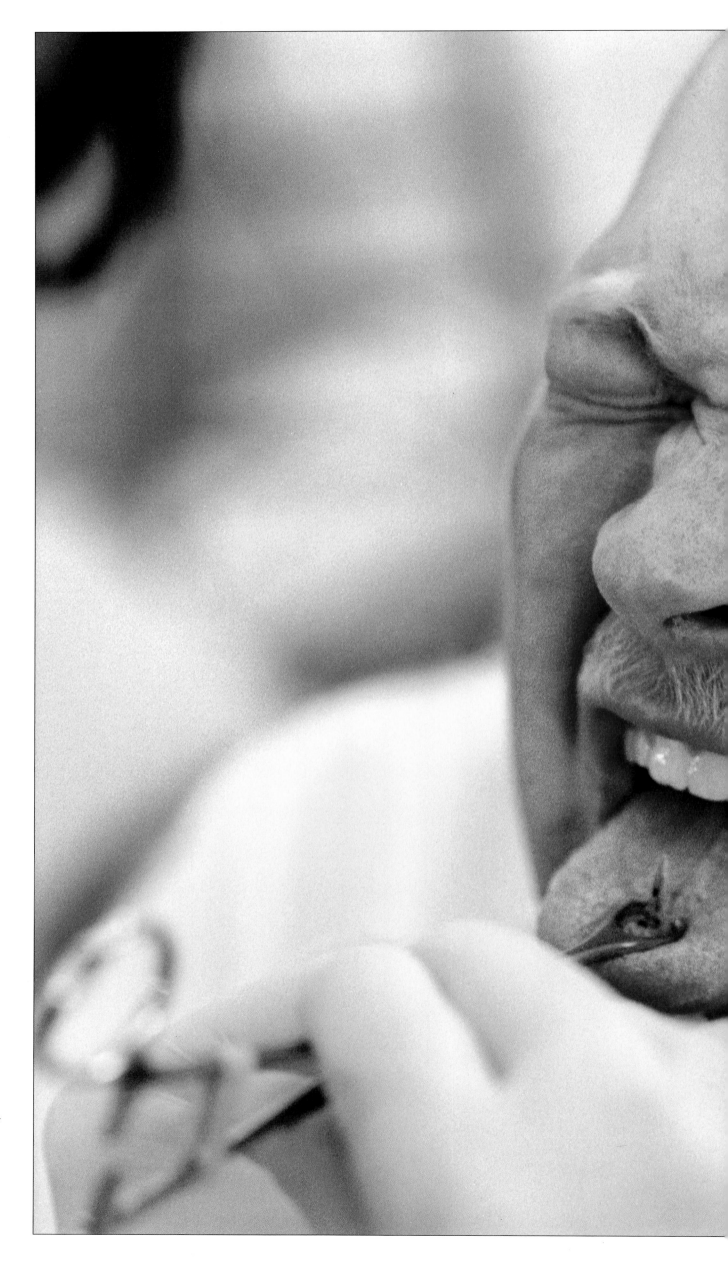

POKING FUN

Mike Reisinger of Highland got his tongue pierced during a riverfront music festival in May. He said it didn't hurt. He said the tongue jewelry, which looks like a barbell, didn't interfere with eating. Or with anything. The piercing and jewelry cost him $30. The 22-year-old truck driver said he planned to keep it. People in nearly all occupations — albeit younger people — got parts of their bodies pierced in 2001. Ears were the most common. Tongues, navels, eyelids and noses were popular pierce points, too. And there were piercings of more intimate body parts as well. Piercing had been a fad for several years. In November 2001, Detroiters elected their first mayor to have a pierced body part: Kwame Kilpatrick, 31 — his left ear lobe. **KENT PHILLIPS**

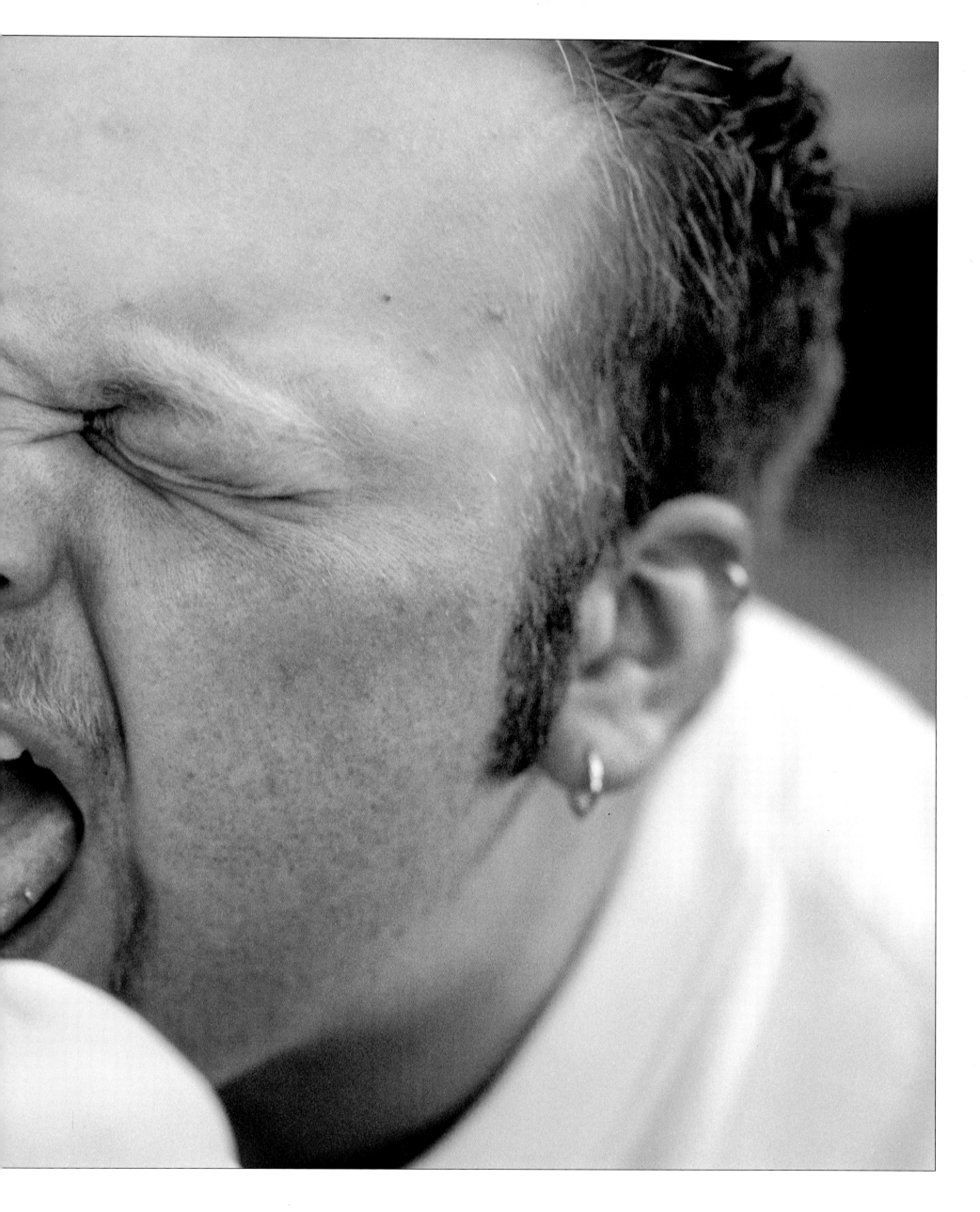

MUSTANG SALLY *(previous page)*

When the first Mustang was made in 1964, it was made at Dearborn Assembly Plant, the final cog of the once-huge Ford Rouge complex. Mustangs continued to churn forth from Dearborn Assembly at a rate of 800 a day in 2001. But the Ford Rouge complex was a shell of what it was after World War I when Henry Ford built the largest industrial complex in the world to take in iron ore at one end and spit out cars at the other. This Mustang body was being spot-welded as it moved along that line. And you don't see many assemblers. Robots had replaced many workers; the economic layoffs that periodically occurred had taken a toll on workers, too. By 2001, the average age of automobile assembly line workers at many area factories was about 50. That Mustang, by the way, sold for about $20,000 fully assembled.

PATRICIA BECK

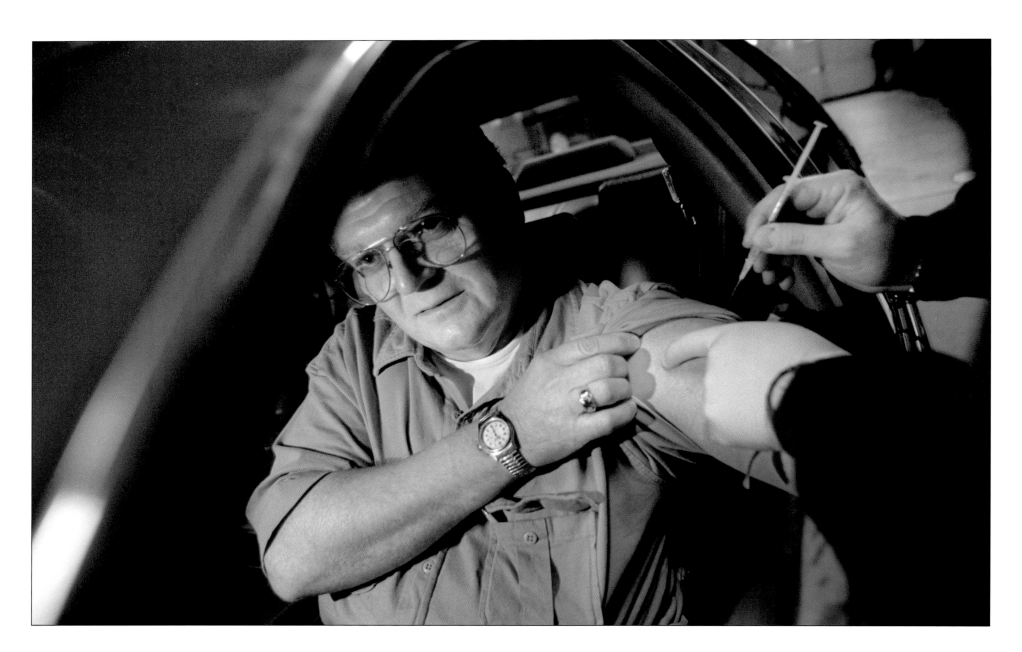

HE FLU RIGHT THROUGH

We seemed to live in our cars. A motorist with the right equipment probably could have lived in a car — except for pit stops. Drive-through services were pervasive in 2001. Douglas Snarski of Goodells got a flu shot from paramedic Wade Gracey without leaving his car. All Snarski had to do was drive up to the garage at Richmond-Lenox Emergency Medical Service in northern Macomb County, roll down his window, and roll up his sleeve. He was on his way in five minutes. Cost, $10. In 2001, the drive-up flu shot program was in its second year and served about 110 people. Sometimes flu season also meant delays in vaccine shipments, or shortages. **CHIP SOMODEVILLA**

WATER OF LIFE

Kim Beneteau, 28, struggled as she prepared to bring another life into the world, via water. With help from Sarah Watson, a doula, or childbirth coach, and husband Todd Beneteau, Kim eventually gave birth to Jacob Andrew Beneteau at 5:15 a.m. Aug. 29, 2001, after 16 hours of labor. She was one of the few women in the United States who opted to give birth without medical intervention — no cesarean section, no IVs, no epidural anesthesia or enemas, no episiotomies, no doctors. Such births were rare. The only independent birthing center that was left in Michigan in 2001 was the Birth Place in Taylor, run by Bridgett Ciupka, a certified professional midwife. Non-nurse midwives like Ciupka were legal and licensed in 16 states; in Michigan, they were legal but unlicensed. Each birth cost $2,700.

MANDI WRIGHT

GREAT GATHERINGS

We got together, rubbed shoulders, shared our causes and our interests in many ways in 2001. Left: The Bal Africain 2001 was an annual event supporting African and African-American art. Held in the Great Hall at the Detroit Institute of Arts, which boasted an extensive collection of African and African-American art, it raised $300,000. The event had been a social must for 38 years. Patrons included (from left) Pat Taylor and her husband, Ford Motor Co. executive Mike Taylor; Roxanne Thomas; Judge Craig Strong; Pam Rodgers, president of Rodgers Chevrolet dealership; General Motors Acceptance Corp. executive Jim Farmer, and Theresa and Roy Green of Northville. Below: For generations, the river drew us. On Memorial Day, members of the Detroit Yacht Club gathered at the Belle Isle facility to remember war veterans. They are (from left) Rear Commodore David Coleman, Vice Commodore Lucius Tripp, Fleet Chaplain the Rev. Russ Koehler and past Commodore Don Baker. The club had held such services since just after the Civil War. In November, the club's 1,200 members elected Tripp, a 59-year-old neurosurgeon from Bingham Farms, commodore — the fleet's first black leader. In 2001, about a third of club members were minorities.

SUSAN TUSA

THE CUSTOMARY MANNERS

The women at left shopped for a wedding gift for a friend who had recently immigrated from Iraq. But Fordous Kareen (left), Hiyam Fathel and Thankaah Ali would not buy the jewelry themselves. Instead, they would report their findings to the bride's husband-to-be, according to custom, so he could make the purchase. Showing the jewelry to the women was Ali Elsayed at his shop in Dearborn. Below: There was a correct way to sit, to stand, to walk, and Maxine Powell (right, wearing a hat) impressed that on her student, Beverly Pollack of Detroit. Powell had taught etiquette to the stars and to Detroit debutantes for 50 years. We had customs, and we had manners; but not all of our customs were good, and there were plenty of rude people, too. Some bad customs and rudeness displayed in 2001: playing car radios too loud, running red lights, swearing in public and littering.

MANDI WRIGHT

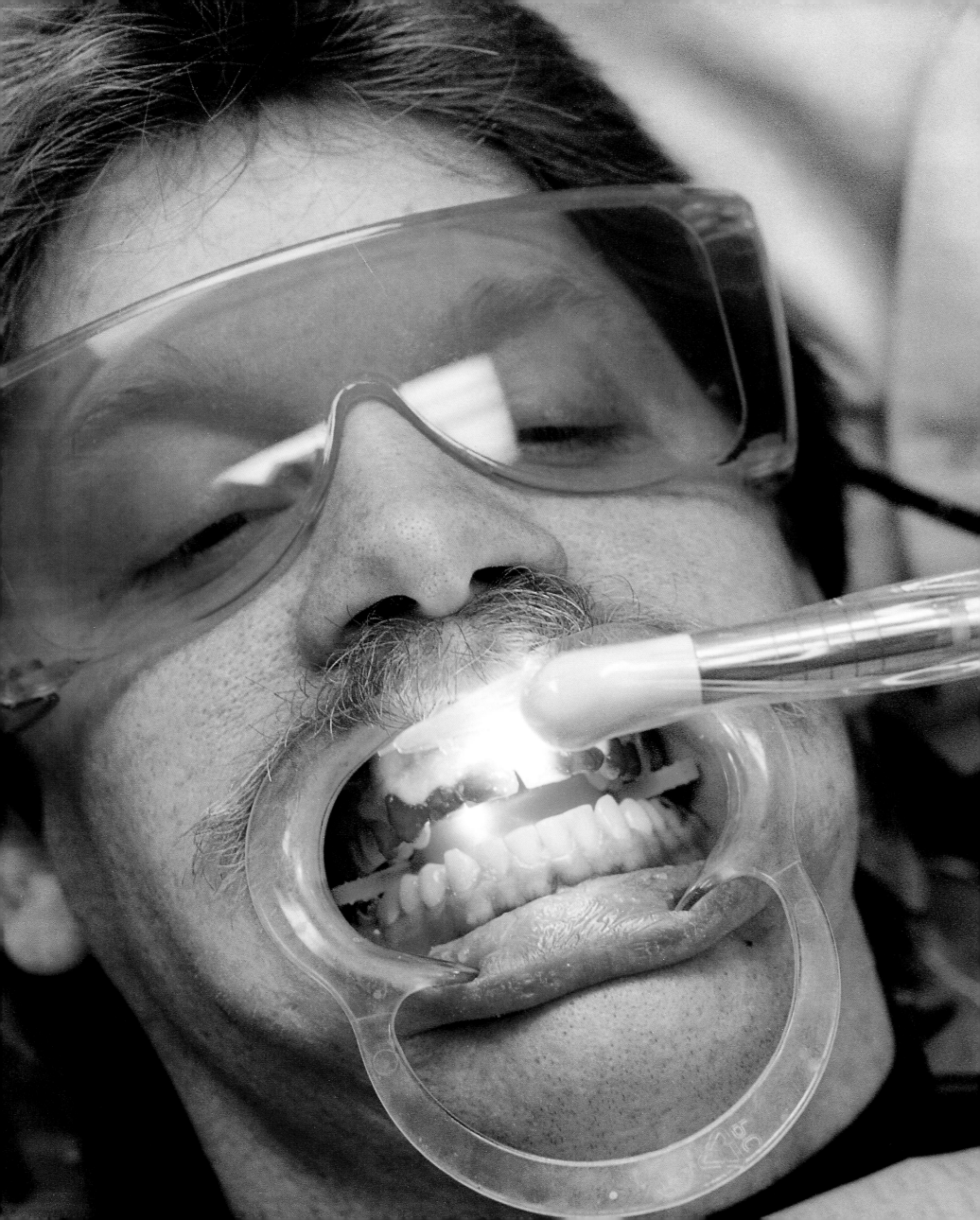

BEING FASHIONABLE

Sometimes the wear said as much about the venue as the person decked to be noticed. And maybe our penchant in 2001 to dress, accessorize, pierce, primp, powder and preen with abandon was our statement that inhibitions were of another era. Tony Palmer of Port Huron stoned his head for a Madonna concert at the Palace in Auburn Hills in August. A Madonna concert and a fan with a rhinestone hairline went hand in hand. Greg Hanna of Jackson and Diana (Dee) Kraus of Farmington (above) came dressed with splash for the annual Fash Bash at the State Theatre on Woodward. The event drew 4,800 people and raised $560,000 for the Detroit Institute of Arts. The State was part of the burgeoning theater district anchored by the Fox Theatre. By 2001, that area was a rejuvenated success story, drawing thousands of mostly young people for weekend and special events.

NECKLINES

Angela Slate of Detroit (bottom) made sure she radiated at Fash Bash. The beads came from 2001's Mardi Gras in New Orleans. That's a Comerica Park light tower behind her. The pros showed up too (below), as the I Group models Sarah Petrere (left) from Hamtramck and Bonnie White from Ferndale worked the Fash Bash crowd. Models in 2001 made about $350 for a six-hour day at major events.

PAUL GONZALEZ VIDELA

J. KYLE KEENER

CAR GUY

John Manuel, in his Brioni tux, posed in front of a Volkswagen at the benefit gala at the North American International Auto Show in January. Manuel came up from Dallas for the event. Cars have lured people to Detroit for 100 years. Most stayed to build them. By 2001, the automobile industry was so global that, even in Detroit, being seen in a Japanese or German car wasn't given a second thought. **J. KYLE KEENER**

HERE, KITTY

A Friday night in October at the Lager House on Michigan Avenue near Tiger Stadium. These were the Intoxicats, a raucous four-piece local rockabilly-punk band. That meant they played country/rock music with attitude. Lyrics were about cars, sin, lust, redemption and life in the Motor City. In 2001, the grungy, unpretentious nightspot was part of the dedicated Detroit music scene.

PAUL GONZALEZ VIDELA

Auto mechanic Earl Richardson from Toledo tried his luck at the MGM Grand Casino in July. In 2001, the three Detroit casinos recorded about $1 billion in revenues — about $1 million a day per casino. We were wondering where the casinos would lead us. Detroit was no Las Vegas, but in 2001 it was the largest city in North America with legalized gambling. Would the casinos spawn myriad social ills? Would they soon draw thousands of tourists who would spend time away from the gaming tables, too? Or would they fade as a fad? $1 billion a year was a lot . . .

PAUL GONZALEZ VIDELA

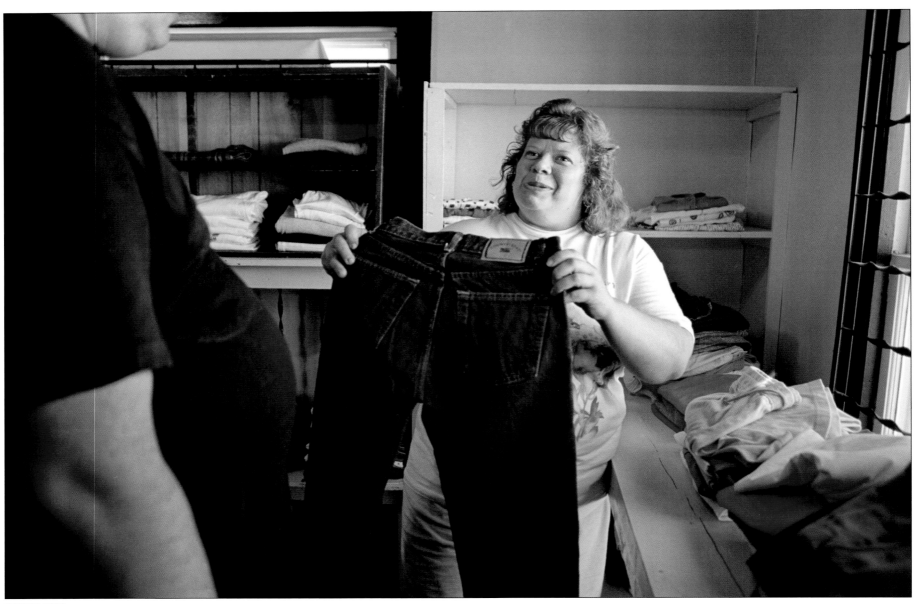

PATRICIA BECK

READY TO WEAR

At Neiman Marcus, an upscale department store at the Somerset Collection in Troy, shoppers could pick up a Louis Feraud jacket for $1,300. If they felt like splurging, there were Giorgio Armani dresses for $3,000. The store's three floors radiated affluence and high style. The store's PR chief, Mimi Shrek, leaned on a rail to take it all in. A tad north in Pontiac — but leagues away in annual revenues — the Baldwin Church and Center's clothing closet gave away donated clothes to the needy. The center helped about 400 people each month, and was overseen by Patty Stephens, left, herself once a beneficiary of the church's services. The center was established in the early 1990s, about the same time as the Neiman Marcus store.

POUNDING
IN THE MESSAGE

We were fat. In 2001, only 3 percent of Michiganders did the four simple things that could make them healthier: control their weight, eat enough fruits and veggies, exercise, and avoid tobacco. Michigan was second in the nation in obesity; three of five people here overtipped the scales by 30 pounds or more. These five people in December learned about fat at Beaumont Rehab and Health Center in Birmingham. Dietitian Suzette Kroll held up a plastic mold representing a pound of human fat. Candace Goss (left), Carole Kody, Tim Brennan, Marilyn Sokolowski and Willis Brown contemplated. **CHIP SOMODEVILLA**

SUSAN TUSA

KENT PHILLIPS

WILLIAM ARCHIE

ERIC SEALS

WILLIAM ARCHIE

THE FLAVORS OF MOTOWN

Metro Detroit was the kind of place where you could graze through a nearly inexhaustible smorgasbord of food. Still, pizza ruled. And Little Caesars dominated. Below left: Angela Harris (right) and coworker Juan Harris hustled the pizzas at a Little Caesars outlet in northwest Detroit. The chain was owned by Mike and Marian Ilitch, who started their business in Garden City in 1959. If pizza got a little boring, you could have tried the traditional Middle Eastern meat pie from the Golden Bakery in Dearborn (far left), much of it made by immigrants from Lebanon, Syria, Iraq and the Palestinian territories — many of whom settled in western Wayne County. Second from left: Sometimes, lunch came through compassion. At the Capuchin Soup Kitchen, an east side Detroit institution since 1929, volunteers dished up hot meals for the needy. Top, second from right: Maria Del Carmen Fuente Maldonado of Detroit prepared cactus leaves. The Detroit area in 2001 had a sizeable Hispanic population. Above: We thought of Hamtramck, and paczki (pronounced POONCH-kee) came to mind. Lisa Sauve bit into the delectable sugary confection, a Polish pastry, at the New Palace Bakery. It was Lisa's first ever taste, and she approved. The doughy jelly-filled treats were prepared for the eve of Lent, as fasting time for Christians. The high-calorie pastries were such a hit in metro Detroit that Fat Tuesday was also hailed as Paczki Day.

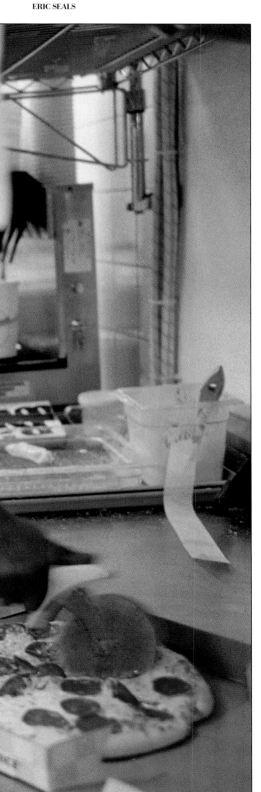

MANDI WRIGHT

AGELESS BEAUTY

Helen Enlow (left) was 86 when she was crowned winner in the annual Ms. Senior American House Regional Pageant in Rochester Hills in February. In 2001, the oldest contestant was 102. Contestants were judged on talent (skills ranged from embroidery to dress-making). Between 1990 and 2000, Michigan's 100-plus population grew by more than 35 percent, to 1,535. Experts projected that number would double every 10 years. Below: Andrea Juarez, 5, from Detroit was a mirror image of sister Rosalia Blackburn, who was having makeup applied for her quinceanera, a celebration among Hispanics of a girl's transition to womanhood at her 15th birthday. Bottom: Carletta Higginbotham, 9, made a final adjustment before leaving for the big dance. Waiting was great-grandfather Douglas Davis, who was taking her to the dance at Thurgood Marshall Elementary in Detroit. The dance was sponsored by Club Marvelous, an after-school program for girls in grades 3-5. Its goals were to expose them to the arts, etiquette, community service and a healthy lifestyle.

CHIP SOMODEVILLA

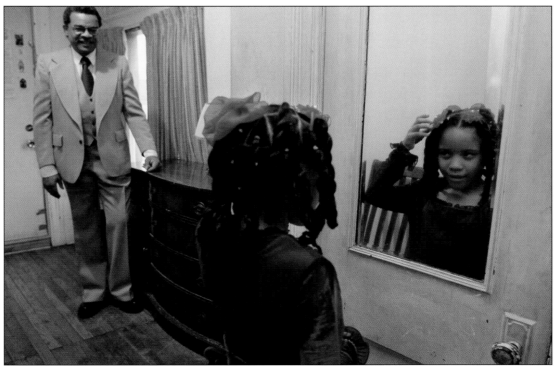

KIRTHMON F. DOZIER

MANY HANDS, ONE AIM

Barn raisings didn't come through Detroit often. And it wasn't easy work. But the students at Catherine Ferguson Academy on the west side wouldn't let a 500-pound beam stop them from chipping in to build a barn for animals at the school's working farm. About 350 students, mostly teen mothers and pregnant young women, were enrolled at the school. There, students experienced the usual rites of high school, and learned about animal care and food production. Child care was also a feature. And who was Catherine Ferguson? Students picked that name, in honor of a woman who was born a slave in 1779 but went on to set up the first Sunday school in New York City. **HUGH GRANNUM**

CLASH OF THE TITANS

Andre Gignac (left) and Pete Maziak showed that it was not all-work-and-no-play at the second annual Michigan Information Technology gathering at Cobo Center in downtown Detroit. They were geared up as sumo wrestlers, using pads and a special suit to pack on the pounds. The game was one of many on display at the 2001 technology event, held when the industry was slumping. In the hallways, as participants schmoozed, networked, swapped business cards, eavesdropped and grabbed freebies, there was talk of a tech rebound. But for a few moments that afternoon, the only rebounding Maziak and Gignac were preoccupied with was off each other. **PATRICIA BECK**

BIG PLANS, SMALL QUARTERS

The township workers probably knew what it felt like to be sardines in a can. They were in the basement of Rose Township's 1,600-square-foot town hall, which they and many residents had long said was too small. In 2001, new municipal facilities were a delicate issue in communities across Michigan because tax-conscious voters wanted to make sure the needs were legit. Smaller offices made sense to many, however, since the high-tech revolution saw computers storing information on wafer-thin disks. The old-fashioned way meant city and township halls needed space for rows of file cabinets. Despite the high-tech stuff, paper — and paperwork — didn't vanish. Many people said they found themselves using and stowing more paper because of computers.
RICHARD LEE

HUGH GRANNUM

TIRED OUT *(previous pages)*

We were never Miami, so on the occasional days when it got very hot, we wilted rapidly. Many of us went to a water park, a fairly recent creation in which machine-made waves gave us that Malibu feel on Melvindale budgets. There were several water parks around the region, all of them swarming — like this one was — with relief seekers on an August day when the temperature hit 96. Electricity usage strained utilities, and officials advised people to raise the temperature settings on their air conditioners to 78 degrees to conserve power. Patrons at Oakland County-operated Red Oaks wave pool in Madison Heights paid about $5 to loll in the water. **WILLIAM ARCHIE**

A CHILD OF FAITH

The Ste. Anne's in southwest Detroit near the Ambassador Bridge is the eighth church building for the parish, which was formed two days after Detroit was founded in 1701. The parish first served the French Catholic community in Detroit. But around World War II, the parish grew more diverse and by the church's and city's 300th anniversary in July, it was a mostly Mexican-American congregation. It is a handsome building — and the resting place of a famous Detroiter, Father Gabriel Richard, who died in 1832. On the day of the church's 300th — July 26 — Elizabeth Taamneh, 7, waited to present a ring of flowers to Cardinal Adam Maida, the archbishop of Detroit. **WILLIAM ARCHIE**

Love was hard, and married life was often a trial of patience and tenacity. Mike Kramer (left) and Joe Kort knew all about love and challenges as they decorated a holiday tree in December 2001. They were married a year earlier. They had weathered arguments with newspaper editors who wouldn't print their engagement announcement because the couple wouldn't call what they had planned a "commitment ceremony." Kort and Kramer insisted that the rites they performed at the dawn of their marriage were nothing short of a full-scale, pull-out-all-the-stops wedding. They faced social pressures and a stigma that cast gay commitments as illegitimate. Like all couples, they experienced joy and they confronted the demons of selfishness and narcissism, insularity and doubt. They overcame many of the challenges, they said, by facing their shortcomings with a healthy dose of compromise. And love.
MANDI WRIGHT

Sometimes it was hard for kids to know when to fight for something and when to walk away, but boxing promoter and manager Andrea Darnell aimed to teach them. Darnell, photographed trading jabs with 11-year-old Vincent Williams at the Detroit Boxing Club on the city's west side, founded a program that trained kids to work hard, be disciplined and reach for a dream — be it getting good grades, learning a fun and challenging sport like boxing or becoming the next Golden Gloves champ. **DAVID P. GILKEY**

MANDI WRIGHT

I DO

At right, mariachi band leader Salvador Torres danced with the bride, Jennifer Gomez, 24, of Romeo, who had known Torres since she was 12. Her groom, Jeffery Hunley, 24, waited his turn. Left, top: Conyey North stood at left, watching groomsman Bill Arrington (center) and his brother Roland whoop it up with honking well-wishers after departing from the wedding ceremony of Antoinette and Jon Hicks on June 23 at the Little Rock Baptist Church on Woodward Avenue in Detroit. Left, bottom: Angelica Martinez, 25, and Rita Daniels, 34, both of Belleville, participated in a June wedding service during PrideFest, an annual gay and lesbian event in Ferndale. Their marriage would not be legally recognized in Michigan. In 2001, Vermont was the only state with a civil union law that granted marriage-like rights to same-sex couples.

RICHARD LEE

ERIC SEALS

HOMECOMING TRADITIONS

Usually in early October, just before you could see your frosty breath, high schools held homecomings, with floats and parades and dances and a regal court. At Eisenhower High School in Shelby Township, during halftime at the homecoming game, Jane Biecker embraced Andrea Rau, 17, as the homecoming court was named. At left, Jessica Biecker, 18, and at right, Liz Mickalich, 17. Usually homecoming drew few alumni save for the previous year's grads. Homecoming was more for the students at school. Eisenhower beat Utica, by the way, 41-7. **JENNIFER HACK**

KIRTHMON F. DOZIER

HUGH GRANNUM

NO PLACE LIKE HOME

Below: In 2001, college students like Jeff Haase were known for their ingenuity. Haase, photographed standing in his dorm room, collaborated with his roommate to make the most of their room at Oakland University in Auburn Hills. The common area had two compact refrigerators and a microwave — more than enough to handle late-night study snacks and parties. Students also built lofts to create what functioned as a second floor — beds above and space for desks, computers and everything else below. Dorm rooms, though usually small, had many comforts of home. Most in Michigan included high-speed Internet access, cable TV and free voice mail. **MANDI WRIGHT**

PATRICIA BECK

PATRICIA BECK

PAUL GONZALEZ VIDELA

ERIC SEALS

OUR DREAM HOMES

From top: Doug Finegood saw a great opportunity to make his decorating dreams come true when his marriage ended. He transformed his three-bedroom Oak Park ranch home into a shrine to his favorite cartoon, the Flintstones (the show was big in the 1960s, and later in syndication). He hired an amateur artist to paint murals. This one shows the Flintstones, the Rubbles, Dino and Gazoo. "Believe it or not, some people think I'm nuts," Finegood said, wearing his favorite Fred Flintstone T-shirt. "But, I just think it's a fun hobby. Nobody leaves my house without a smile on their face."

Ever since she was a little girl, Sheila Starnes of Southfield dreamed of living in a contemporary home like the one she saw one day while driving with her mom. Years later, she saw the home advertised for sale, and convinced her husband to check it out with her. "We weren't thinking of moving," Starnes said. "But I fell in love with it all over again."

An invitation to computer buffs turned this Wyandotte home into a computer wonderland in October. Justin Garcia was the last to fall asleep at the all-night networking party. His friend had asked him and others to bring over their computer systems — Garcia tucked his custom-designed machine into a small suitcase — so they could all be hooked up to play games and share files for hours.

Philip Schnepp's dreams were dashed when he and his family were driven from their $400,000 home in Northville Township by black mold that was making them all sick. Unable to leave his dream home behind for good, though, he came back from time to time to pick up odds and ends, and to lament the loss of some possessions — possessions like this dress. His daughter liked to tap dance in it, but couldn't anymore because it was contaminated by the airborne mold that scarred his wife's lungs and forced him to wear a protective mask.

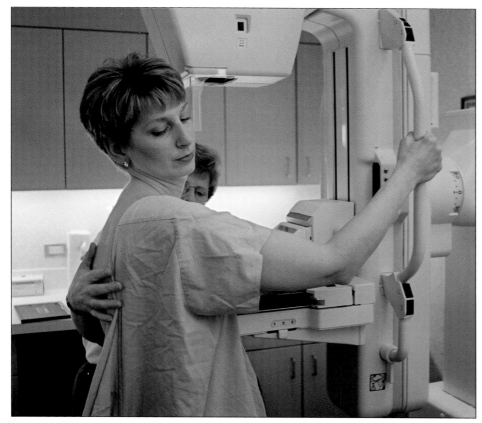

PATRICIA BECK

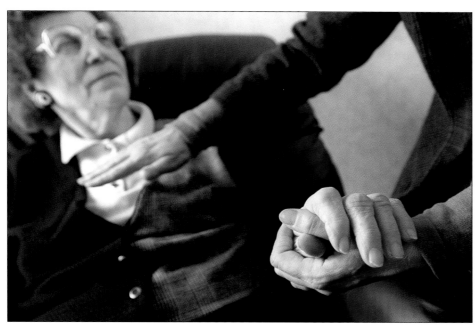

HUGH GRANNUM

GABRIEL B. TAIT

TREATING OUR AILMENTS

At left, Lisa Whitcomb, 34, got a baseline mammogram in April at William Beaumont Hospital in Royal Oak. Lucy Blumm helped her get into position. Doctors planned to use it for comparison when Whitcomb had annual screening mammograms later in life. Federal guidelines suggested that annual mammograms should begin at age 40. Whitcomb's test cost about $220. In 2001, 6,800 Michigan women were diagnosed with breast cancer; 1,400 died of it. Mammography is an X-ray image of the breast. Since 1950, it had reduced breast cancer deaths by at least 25 percent among women ages 50 to 70. The equipment was expensive; the machine Blumm operated used film and cost about $80,000. Digital mammography machines reduced exam times and helped doctors read mammograms better, but cost at least $400,000.

Center: Some health maintenance organizations, or HMOs, offered subsidies on alternative health treatments — among them acupuncture, massage therapy and nutrition counseling. At the St. John Health System's Life Enhancement Center in St. Clair Shores, Helen Wyszomierski of St. Clair Shores was treated using Reiki, a spiritually based healing technique that relies on the the placement of hands and the body's natural energies.

Below: His name, Martez Applewhite. He was 3 and he was screaming because nurse Rebecca Mullin at Children's Hospital of Michigan was giving him a shot. We had come a long way medically, but in 2001, it was still painful for a little boy to get a shot. Martez was undergoing a series of 30 shots over 5 days in a process to purge heavy metals, like lead, from his system.

NAVIGATING THE RENCEN

The interior of the Renaissance Center had been called maddening and magnificent, awe-inspiring and awful, a work of art and a rat's maze. The complex was General Motors Corp.'s world headquarters, situated by the banks of the Detroit River. Its exterior — shiny glass-and-metal cylinders — made it the most recognizable complex on Detroit's cityscape. But some visitors remarked that its interior, dominated by corridors and hallways linking the towers, could be a challenge, although some innovations — such as the steel-and-glass circulation ring — were de-

signed to simplify pedestrian traffic. The ring was part of the $500-million remake of the complex. GM bought the RenCen in 1996 for $75 million. Among other projects in the remodeling: a giant glass house and a restaurant atop the 73-story hotel tower. J. KYLE KEENER

WHERE THE WATERS KISS

Where the Rouge met the Detroit, a fishing boat negotiated the currents and the flow. This eerie effect was caused because the Rouge had a higher amount of sediment and a slower rate of flow. Anglers claimed this spot was a bonanza for catching fish. We were pleased at the clarity and limited pollution of the Detroit River in 2001 — a far cry from the mid-20th Century when few people fished the river and even fewer dared wade into it. **DAVID P. GILKEY**

HORNS AND ANTLERS

In his studio near Fowlerville in Livingston County, taxidermist Jerry Deaven worked to turn hunters' trophies into art. That stuffed bear behind him was one. Hunting was big in Michigan: In 2001, an estimated 750,000 firearms hunters killed almost 300,000 deer during the November season. But a dark side also emerged, and affected folks like Deaven. It seemed that theft of antlers was also becoming prevalent. Deaven lost 25 sets of white-tail antlers, each worth $50-$100. The antlers were used in arts and crafts, fashioned into candleholders, knife handles, gun racks, even chandeliers — a 10-bulb specimen could cost $1,300. Ground up antler was also touted as an aphrodisiac. **PATRICIA BECK**

REFLECTING ON THE CATCH

Denard Nelson checked his line and the current as Andrew Foster held up his catch, a sheepshead, at a fishing spot near Historic Ft. Wayne in Detroit. Other popular catches in 2001: perch, bass and walleye. If you didn't have access to a boat, there were numerous public fishing piers. The most popular: Belle Isle and Riverside Park. **DAVID P. GILKEY**

RICHARD LEE

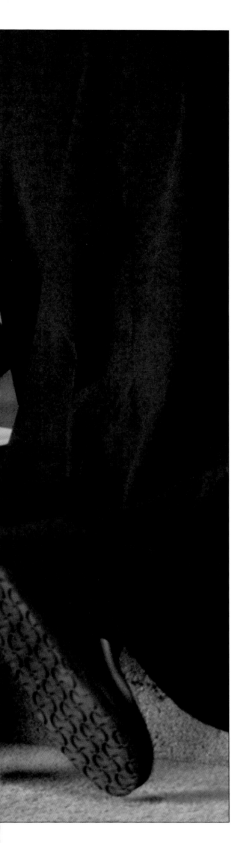

ANIMALS IN SERVICE

Destiny, a golden retriever puppy, showed her devotion at the altar of St. John's Episcopal Church in Royal Oak during communion in January. Attending services with their trainers helped some dogs prepare to fulfill their ultimate destiny: to help sight-impaired people. Above: Some camels would walk a mile for a person. Debbi Steenbergh waved as daughter Michele (back seat) and grandchildren (from front) Michael Duquet, 3, Jessica DeHate, 5, and Samantha DeHate, 3, clumped along on Clyde the Camel. They paid $3 for the five-minute camel ride outside a Toys R Us store in Roseville in July. Camels weren't often found in Michigan. Most kids — even in 2001 — still craved the coin-operated mechanical horse ride usually found at entrances to discount stores.

AN EMBLEM OF OUR PAST

Nellie Toler, 104, was born to Mississippi sharecroppers in 1897. For years, she hefted bags of cotton for 50 cents a day to support her three children. At age 59, she came to Detroit to live with her son and his family, got her high school diploma and found work at a city recreation center. She retired at age 101. City officials honored her determination with a standing ovation at a special Detroit 300th birthday breakfast in 2001. That year, she spent most of her time looking after the younger generations in her family, like great-great-granddaughters Jazzmin, right, and Shanavia Thomas. J. KYLE KEENER

MENTOR IN THE MIDDLE

Thousands of kids in Detroit didn't have the company or the guidance of an adult. Many of them spent long stretches of their days on their own, or with other kids. And that's where mentoring came in. It was popular in the 1990s, and medical studies showed that teens with mentors were less likely than those without to engage in risky behaviors such as using drugs and carrying weapons. Harold White was one such mentor, helping Eugene Wooten, 12, right, while Eugene's brother George, 11, left, took a break. White belonged to Second Grace United Methodist Church, which with First United, teamed up to mentor kids from Dixon Elementary. Most of Dixon's students lived below the poverty line. The program helped more than 300 children. **HUGH GRANNUM**

THE TONE OF THE TIMES

Some of us went to nightclubs like Space at 415 E. Congress downtown. It had four differently themed floors. Its exterior sported a shiny silver beacon. Inside, the thump of electronic music was ever-present, the dance floor and chill-out room were filled with patrons who weren't afraid to get very neighborly and psychics, dwarf wrestlers and dominatrices all regularly held court. On busy weekends, 4,000 patrons flocked to Space. They paid $10 to enter at 10 p.m., and $20 at midnight. Space closed at 4:30 a.m. Many of us did not go to nightclubs like Space. But in 2001, what made Space special was that it was thriving, and so was much of downtown Detroit. After a generation of silence, downtown was again an entertainment destination. We were anxious to see where that would lead. **PAUL GONZALEZ VIDELA**

KIRTHMON F. DOZIER

CHIP SOMODEVILLA

PAUL GONZALEZ VIDELA

MANDI WRIGHT

OUR FEEL FOR THE MUSIC

The world in 2001 celebrated Detroit as the music city. For decades, Detroit was synonymous with the Motown sound. But by 2001, the accolades included electronic music, rappers and new acts with versions of rock and alternative sounds. The city could brag about a rich gospel tradition and in the spring held an awesome country music festival at Hart Plaza. Above: Kenny Larkin performed for a sellout crowd at St. Andrews Hall in Detroit during the Detroit Electronic Music Festival in May. The weekend event brought 1 million fans to concerts downtown. Upper right: The Temptations' Barrington Henderson performed in concert. The group was a Motown headliner for decades. Right: Meg White of the White Stripes in concert at the Rivera Court in the Detroit Institute of Arts in November. She and Jack White, from southwest Detroit, formed the duo that became more famous in Europe in 2001 than it was here. Bottom: Fans of local band the Ruiners ruin kitchen appliances during a performance at the Hamtramck Blowout/Mid by Midwest Music Festival in March. Sort of fan-participatory music.

HOMETOWN HEADLINERS

Right: The Material Girl herself, Madonna, in concert at the Palace in Auburn Hills in August. A product of Oakland County, she became world famous with her cleverly marketed brand of music punctuated by her uninhibited lifestyle. Below, from top: Eminem, Kid Rock, Aretha Franklin. We'll start with Marshall Mathers, a.k.a. Eminem, of Macomb County. He appeared in a Mt. Clemens court in this April photo to answer a gun charge. The judge gave him two years of probation. Eminem was a rapper who reveled in raunchy, misogynist lyrics. He had millions of fans nationally. Kid Rock, from Romeo, rivaled Eminem in popularity and performed with lots of flash. Aretha Franklin grew up in Detroit singing gospel at New Bethel Baptist Church, where her famous father C.L. Franklin was pastor. By 2001, after a 40-year music career, she had become one of the country's top pop music divas. **MANDI WRIGHT,** *right*

JOHN COLLIER

KIRTHMON F. DOZIER

KENT PHILLIPS

A CELL OF SURVIVORS

*With their cell phones at the ready, four Oakland County men
who survived the Sept. 11 attacks on the World Trade Center
waited in a room near a local television studio stage where they
were to recall the horror. Amos Sheena, 28, (left), David Halibu,
25, Fawzi Nona, 29, and Ronei Foumia, 25, (far right) were
working on the 83rd floor of the north tower in Halibu's Naneva
Capital stock trading company. (The man second from right was
not identified) All four were Chaldean-American friends who grew
up in Oakland County communities. After the tower was struck,
they and other employees fled down 82 flights of stairs, passing
firefighters going up. The firefighters would be killed when the
tower collapsed. We heard and recalled hundreds of stories from
survivors and spent the days after 9/11 sharing our own tales with
friends: "Where were you when you heard about the attack?" And
cell phones, which were pervasive by 2001, became the links many
of us used to share our tales. During the attack, people on board
the ill-fated planes and in the World Trade Center towers also
communicated by cell phones with loved ones. For many, the calls
were their last contact.* **KENT PHILLIPS**

WHAT WAS IN A NAME

In the weeks that followed Sept. 11, Americans became aware that Osama bin Laden and numerous Muslim extremist clerics had called on their followers to engage in a jihad, or holy war, against the United States. The word took on threatening connotations, although in Islamic tradition it had been used to refer to an internal struggle for self-improvement or to overcome temptations. By that meaning, every Muslim is supposed to practice jihad. Metro Detroit Muslims shared with Free Press journalists their personal jihads in late 2001. And a few of the 100 Michigan residents who were named Jihad shared their thoughts on their names. Gehad Al-Hadidi, 18, of West Bloomfield was photographed in the living room of his family's home. **PATRICIA BECK**

ADJUSTING TO A NEW LIFE

Pashke Palucaj, an Albanian American living in Rochester Hills, prayed every day that her daughter, Rita Gjergjaj, would be found safe and alive. She set up this shrine at home after Rita, 30, vanished Feb. 25 and her abusive ex-husband fled the country. "In America, we have different cultures and it's hard to put it together," Albanian American Martin Camaj said. Albanians were among the more than 140 different ethnic groups that settled in Detroit. Like many other groups, most of the Albanians came here after 1960. And like most groups that had been migrating to Detroit since the early 1800s, traditions and customs from the old country sometimes clashed with new world culture. Men from some patriarchal ethnic groups refused to recognize female authority, which often caused problems for female teachers or police officers. As 2001 ended, Rita Gjergjaj's fate remained unknown.
MANDI WRIGHT

A DAVID VS. GOLIATH CRASH

In Grosse Pointe Park, the driver of a sport-utility vehicle collided with a car. The SUV wound up on its side. Even as they became among the most popular vehicles on the road, debate stirred about the practicality of SUVs. Consumers loved them for their commanding views, crash safety, versatility and — with four-wheel drive — ability to go through snow. Critics panned them as fuel-chugging menaces to occupants of smaller, lighter vehicles. In 2001, half of the 17.4 million new vehicles consumers bought were light trucks, SUVs, pickups and minivans. **J. KYLE KEENER**

CITY DROPS POLICE

Suffocating beneath $11 million in short-term debt, Highland Park, a city with an operating budget of only $13 million, laid off its police force in December. State police and the Wayne County Sheriff's Department provided police protection for the city of 17,000. The cost-cutting move was implemented by Ramona Pearson, the emergency financial manager appointed by Gov. John Engler a few months earlier to help revive the fiscally floundering city. Sgt. Patrick McClelland, at left, neatly hung his uniform after 27 years of service. Sgt. Bill McLean, at right, with over 33 years of service, came to turn in his cap. **PATRICIA BECK**

ARAB-AMERICAN LIFE

In the days and weeks that followed the horrific Sept. 11 terrorist attacks, Arab Americans were the targets of discrimination. Two months after the attacks, U.S. Assistant Attorney General Ralph Boyd Jr. visited Dearborn, the city with the nation's most prevalent Arab-American population, to address concerns. Imad Hamad, regional director of the American Arab Anti Discrimination Committee, bottom right, listened as people asked questions. Also pictured (from left) are Mario Fundarski and Nancy Unis, both of Dearborn, and Manny Dembs of West Bloomfield.

CHIP SOMODEVILLA

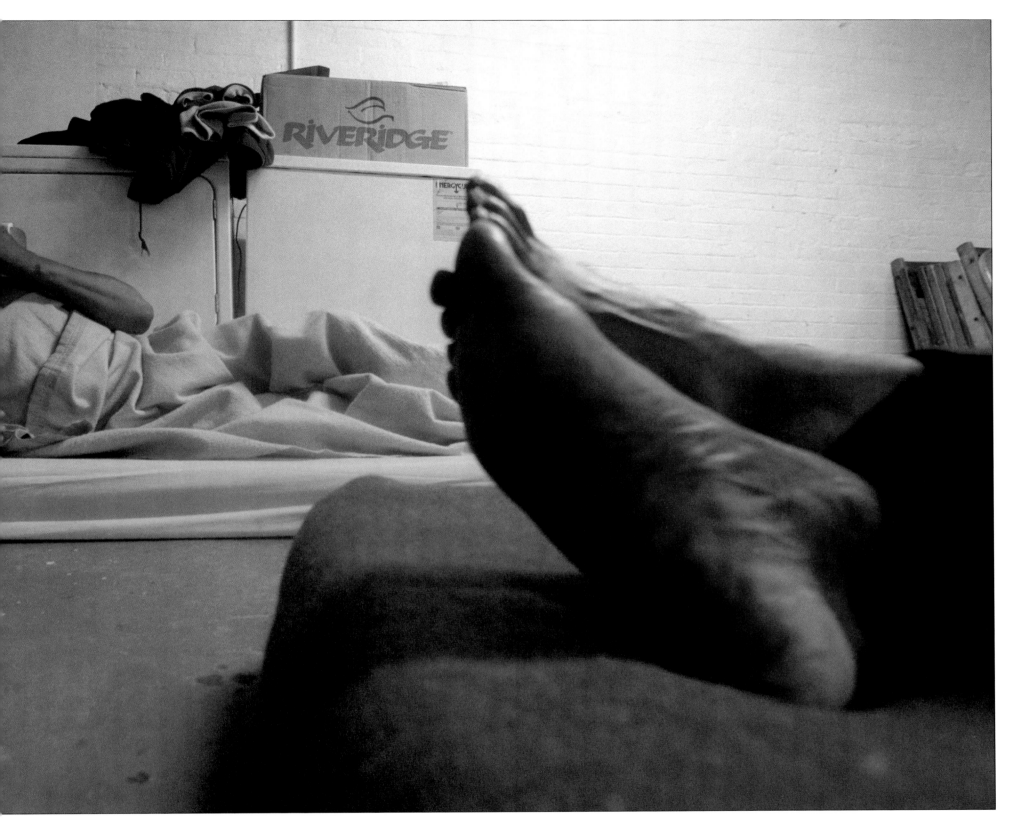

ON THE CITY'S STREETS

With the late-October temperatures below freezing, Bruce Smith (left) was grateful to be indoors. He settled in beneath a thin blanket on the basement floor of the Open Door Rescue Mission at 3442 McDougall in Detroit. The mission had been operating in the city for at least 35 years, according to its executive director, Pastor Jerome Farris. It typically sheltered 35 men a night, but on especially cold nights, it would shelter far more. This night, more than 50 men curled up in pews and on spaces along the floor.
KENT PHILLIPS

AT WORK, FOR A PLAYGROUND

Volunteerism had a hand in the birth and building of playgrounds that dot the metro Detroit area. One such play area took shape on a lot on Hazelwood near the urban New Center neighborhood. The project, with help from volunteers of the Romulus Marriott, was the second for Greening of Detroit, an organization that boosted tree plantings and park creation in Detroit. Jill Robinson, Greening of Detroit's project manager, said the playground on Hazelwood was an astounding success. In 2001, equipment was in place and plans for a brick path were afoot. And even better, she said: The entire neighborhood chipped in to care for and maintain the playground. **MANDI WRIGHT**

BREAKFAST CLUB

*Joe Siefman never had to worry about eating alone in the mornings. At
the Senate Coney Island and Restaurant in Livonia, he enjoyed the company — and the assistance — of direct care worker Sharron Nicholson.
They had known each other for five years. Nicholson often had breakfast
with Siefman at the Senate and took him on short excursions. Among the
stops: a car dealership so he could look at autos. Siefman was an original
resident at the Grantland Home, one of Michigan's first group homes in
1980. In the late 1980s, he retired from a job doing light assembly work,
but kept busy with a twice-weekly paper route. As state institutions
began closing in the 1980s, Grantland Home was established on the
premise that people with developmental disabilities should be entrusted to
the care of the communities in which they live and be allowed to live in
the least restrictive environment.* **PATRICIA BECK**

THE FAITHFUL FARMER

Donald Staebler's parents bought this spread in eastern Washtenaw County for $8,000 when he was a baby. And since then — 90 years ago — the 87-acre farm had been the only home he'd known. Twice daily, he'd haul bales of hay to feed his 45 head of cattle. His farm was among the last in the region. But unlike farms that were developed for housing or commercial use to satisfy urban sprawl, Staebler's farm was sold to Washtenaw County for $1.5 million. Staebler made sure the land would remain unchanged — as a county park. And he cut a deal that allowed him to remain on the farm until his death. Real estate experts said in January that Staebler could have made $2.5 million off the land had he sold it to developers. Staebler responded then that he didn't need the money. **SUSAN TUSA**

A BIG-HOUSE BOOM

The view from above a housing development in Rochester Hills, north of Tienken Road and east of Sheldon, in early December. Huge homes like these were a mini-rage in 2001, continuing a pattern that began in the mid-1990s as the U.S. economy and stock market brought wealth to many Americans. The low mortgage rates helped, too. Six-percent rates propelled sales of new homes in the United States to 900,000 in 2001, breaking the record of 886,000 sold in 1998. Pulte Homes Inc. of Bloomfield Hills was the nation's biggest home builder. It posted impressive profits for 2001, up 38 percent to $302.4 million. The average selling price of homes reached $225,000, compared with the previous year's $206,000. And new home sales spurred other markets, from carpeting and home-improvement stores to landscaping companies. **MANDI WRIGHT**

A SAMPLE OF THINGS TO COME

If you were planning to redo the kitchen, you'd get samples of counters. Paint the den a new shade, ditto on color samples. Put up a world headquarters in downtown Detroit — in 2001, you'd get facade samples. In 2001's spring, workers constructing the Compuware world headquarters at downtown's Campus Martius displayed this facade sample and leaned some exterior skin samples against it to compare and contrast. Which won out? The facade went up in 2002, so you'll need to visit the building to find out. **NANCY ANDREWS**

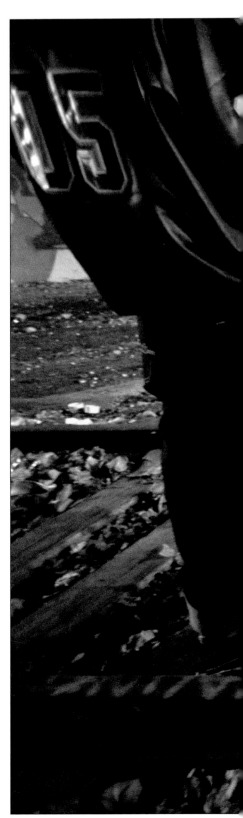

KIRTHMON F. DOZIER

MANDI WRIGHT

PATRICIA BECK

KENT PHILLIPS

KENT PHILLIPS

J. KYLE KEENER

A COMMUNITY ON ALERT

Linda Frederick, top left, was a mail handler for Macomb County. During the anthrax scare, which hit in October, she wore protective gloves and a mask to shield her from the potentially deadly powder. The concern was legitimate: Five people died from inhaling anthrax and more than a dozen were treated for anthrax-related illnesses — most of them postal workers or people who handled mail. Authorities said they believed terrorists sent the deadly bacterium through the mail. Top right: We were cavalier about security before 9/11, but no-nonsense after. Companies across the region passed out identification tags to employees, or strictly enforced policies that workers display ID tags. Those at right are for employees at Million Air, a charter airline in Oakland County. Above, left: Marla was trained to sniff for explosives. She was photographed on Sept. 11, sniffing in what was the soon-to-be-demolished Smith Terminal at Metro Airport. Airport Police Officer Rich Frederick gave Marla orders. Above: From the skies over Afghanistan, a long-anticipated war was waged. It was Oct. 7, 2001. The first strikes opened a sobering chapter in global conflict and unnerved many Americans, who feared retaliation. The FBI put law enforcement agencies across the nation on the highest alert. Detroiter Andrezej Sikora, 44, pictured at left facing the TVs, had taken his car in for service at the Sears department store in Roseville that Sunday afternoon. He stood glued to the TV while waiting for the mechanics to finish the work. A recorded interview with suspected terrorist Osama bin Laden was broadcast. Bin Laden had already been named the United States' leading suspect in the Sept. 11 attacks. Left: A telephone in the Oakland County Emergency Operations center. The system could warn 1 million residents through 205 sirens. Left, below: When an unknown white powder was mailed to Porsche Engineering in Troy, the building was evacuated. The country was on edge over anthrax. But none was found in Troy, or anywhere in metro Detroit.

INDUSTRIAL SHIMMER

Steel mills and power plants south of the Ambassador Bridge had for decades received raw materials from ships using the river. Their discharge of smoke and steam gave the river a ghostly shimmer. But the river's promise of an abundance of fresh water had given many in 2001 confidence that Detroit's life in the future was secure. Would the great migration to the nation's Southwest ebb — indeed reverse to the Great Lakes states — if water becomes expensive and scarce? Yes, we thought. Would industry locate to where the water is when demand far out-strips supply? Yes. "In 100 years, I can easily see a qualified re-industrialization of the Great Lakes," said Mike Donahue, in 2001 the executive director of the Great Lakes Commission. If water shortages develop elsewhere, "the Great Lakes and the Detroit River will be rediscovered."
DAVID P. GILKEY

OLD MODEL CADILLAC
(next page)

Like we did when Detroit turned 200 and 250, part of the city's July 24 birthday cel-ebration included a guy dressed as Antoine de la Mothe Cadillac re -enacting the landing of 1701. (In 1701, Cadillac stepped ashore roughly at the site of what would be the Joe Louis Arena.) Guy Vaneboncoeur from Montreal, Canada, played Cadillac. And Detroiters turned out with cameras to record the accomplishment. It was a hot day, too, so Cadillac was probably anxious to retire to some air-conditioned lounge for a cold Vernors or Faygo. A Cadillac statue was unveiled this day. Earlier in tricentennial celebrations, a 3,000-foot riverfront promenade was opened. **PATRICIA BECK**

OUR ARAB HERITAGE

*Amr Moussa, in the foreground, was secretary general of the Arab
League in 2001. He visited Detroit to announce that his organization
would appoint a liaison with Arab Americans to work on social and
economic issues. That was major news for the burgeoning Arab
American community here. Moussa's Arab League represented 22
countries. Metro Detroit began to welcome Arab immigrants around
1890. Numbers swelled with the advent of the auto industry and again
in the late 1960s. By 2001, estimates suggested that at least 200,000
Arab Americans lived in metro Detroit and that 10,000 of them operated
small businesses. Local leaders in 2001 expressed hope that Detroit would
soon become the gateway for U.S. commerce with the Middle East.*
PATRICIA BECK

THE MOVERS AND SHAKERS

They were due for a good time. The year 2001 had been a rough one for Detroit politicians. The city's ambassador, Mayor Dennis Archer — out at a winter gala with son Dennis Jr., left, and political successor Kwame Kilpatrick, right — decided to call it quits after eight years of working to revitalize neighborhoods, build on regional relationships and improve city departments and services. And Kilpatrick won his shot at running the nation's 10th-largest city only after a bitter contest against City Council President Gil Hill. Archer kept mum about his pick at first, but it became clearer after the race when he met with Kilpatrick — who at 31 was the city's youngest elected mayor — to offer words of wisdom. Alas, the love didn't flow both ways: 2 months later, Kilpatrick would blast Archer's administration in his State of the City address.

CHIP SOMODEVILLA

GOOD TIMES PUT IN PARK

Faced with a lot of unsold inventory like these Chrysler Sebring and Dodge Stratus models, DaimlerChrysler AG announced in January that it would cut 20 percent of the workforce at its U.S. division, the Auburn Hills-based Chrysler Group, over a 3-year period. News of more cuts came in February. Ford Motor Co. also took a hit in 2001. It lost millions by adopting General Motors Corp.'s "Keep America Rolling" campaign, which offered car buyers zero-percent interest rates to help jump start the economy after the Sept. 11 attacks. Incidentally, GM was the only one of metro Detroit's major automakers to come out on top in 2001. For the first time in a decade, it gained in market share. Prior to 2001, the auto industry had enjoyed five strong years. The impact of the slowdown affected all of the businesses that benefited from the area's auto-driven economic boom. **ERIC SEALS**

SEEKING OUR SLIVER OF LAND

Many of us — fed up with office complexes, congested streets, shopping malls and bright lights that blocked out the stars — moved farther north and west, searching for more affordable homes and more green spaces. Ironically, this just added to the problems associated with sprawl. Some areas, like this mobile-home park north of East Avon Road and west of John R in Rochester Hills, were cramped because there was so little land left to park or build on. More than 14,000 new single-family homes were constructed in metro Detroit in 2001, down 26 percent from a 30-year high of 18,831 in 1998. **MANDI WRIGHT**

SWEET TOOTH, SEASON'S RITES

For many, fall meant football. And for Waterford's Mott and Kettering high schools, the gridiron season was ushered in with the Beef Bowl, an annual pregame rite that dated to the late 1990s. The football teams and cheerleading and pompon squads would square off at the Lion's Den Restaurant in Waterford for dinner — and a prime rib eating contest. Two players from each football team would try to polish off 40 ounces of meat. Kettering won in 2001. The young women got in on the fierce competition, too: Mott's Lyndsee Cadieux (left), Devon Heltsley, Sonia Velez and Monica Hall took part in what could be called the cake-eating face-off. They made a mess, but Mott won. **MANDI WRIGHT**

NO PAINT, NO GAIN

Metro Detroiters looking for outdoor action that was more brisk than a hike in the woods rolled running, trekking, and the thrill of the hunt into one activity: paintball. Pro teams like Detroit Fusion finessed strategy and tactics at locations like Paintball World in Warren. As they hid behind their inflatable cover, the players tried to evade a rival team, eliminate the foes or capture the flag, which was in enemy territory. Along the way, through stealth, speed and strategy, the players had to avoid getting spattered by paint pellets that zipped at them at 200 m.p.h. Some players said the adrenaline rush was so intense that they didn't even feel the sting of a pellet when it struck them. A case of 2,000 paintballs cost about $60. The sport's products began to become widely available in metro Detroit in the mid-1990s. In 2001, southeast Michigan was home to at least six paintball fields. With their paint guns and ski masks, players also sometimes brought attitude: Ford Motor Co. employees wore shirts that read, "TANGO — This Ain't No Golf Out." **KENT PHILLIPS**

TREADING GENTLY

The animatronic parasaurolophus was eased to its stand at the Detroit Zoo in April to prepare for thousands of zoo patrons who attended the popular Dinosauria III exhibit. For $12, patrons could tour both the zoo and visit the special exhibit of 20 mechanical dinosaurs that reenacted the moves made by real dinosaurs millions of years ago. Dinosaurs had fascinated us for decades, but in the 1990s and into the 21st Century, people — especially children — devoured information on the extinct creatures. **PATRICIA BECK**

TREADING IN DEEP WATER

Like prehistoric sea beings, David Patterson (left), Cory Kuklewski and Ken Steil surfaced after a practice dive off Belle Isle in May. They were members of the Detroit Police underwater-recovery team who worked regular beats when not called to diving service. What was to recover? Evidence. For generations, the river had been a hiding place for tools of crime. Reflecting the diversity of tasks, Detroit Police included a harbormaster unit, an aviation unit, a canine unit and a bomb-disposal unit. It even had a tug-of-war team and a four-piece band called the Blue Pigs. In 2001, the police force numbered about 4,000. **DAVID P. GILKEY**

FOR POSTERITY *(next pages)*

The western end of Belle Isle . . . a summer day . . . the magnificent skyline in the background . . . the video camera at the ready. We recorded lots of video in 2001, although the latest DVD technology left many wondering what we would do with all that videotape. On this July day, thousands of Detroiters flocked to the riverfront to watch and record a parade of tall ships celebrating the city's tricentennial. That white tent across the river is Chene Park, a popular outdoor concert venue in the summer. **HUGH GRANNUM**

On summer days, like this one in late June, you could see heat rise in shimmering waves from Woodward's asphalt. Cars usually ignored the 35 m.p.h. speed limit; 45 was more like it. Light pole banners, like those celebrating the Detroit Symphony Orchestra, were a city standard. The trend began in the early 1990s; institutions celebrating an anniversary would ask the city to install the banners. The DSO banners were appropriate here because Orchestra Hall was just at the right — and this view was weeks before construction of the north wing to the 1919 facility. Most of the buildings pictured were built before 1930 — save the First Federal Building (late 1960s) dead ahead and the neo-Gothic One Detroit Center on the left (1990s). In 2001 at Campus Martius, the world headquarters for the software company Compuware was being built. Note the construction crane. Ford Field, which was to open in 2002, and Comerica Park, which opened in 2000, stood just left of the church steeples. **PATRICIA BECK**

MERICANS had gone nearly 60 years since the last evil, surprise strike that welded us into a determined people. On Sept. 11, several new generations found so suddenly what earlier ones had discovered Dec. 7, 1941:

Anger can be expressed in tears.

Courage is spontaneous and consumes the timid, too.

Unity? It was always there, in that word after our old world heritage, *hyphen* American.

The American flag united us. Steadfast, brilliant, colors speaking of a heritage that always puts hope first.

And patriotism became a balm we all shared. Spread as thickly or thinly as we wanted, it was still for most of us red, white and blue.

Detroit was no different from the rest of the country when what was normal before the attacks changed into something new.

We stood in lines — some of us for hours — to buy American flags. We put flag decals on our cars and taped paper flags to our windows. We wore flag caps and shirts and shorts and painted our faces with stars and stripes. We wanted to do *something* to strike at the terror that so stunned us, and in one immense, elegant, serendipitous response, we did exactly the thing that needed to be done: Out of many, we became one. *E pluribus unum.*

It would be decades before our zeal to live free of terror will have had its final chapter. We believe — we hope — today that that outcome will favor us mightily.

People tomorrow may well look back on the waning months of 2001 and see us as just what America and its Detroit should have been. Scared, yes; we watched our backs, we scrutinized much. Fearful, no; we got on with our lives.

United, yes; all you needed to do was look and see the unity in flag displays everywhere.

OUT OF MANY, ONE

After Sept. 11, we embraced our myriad cultures more fervently, celebrated our faiths more frequently and drew strength as a community — unified, determined, secure. At Tapestry of Faith Gatherings in October in Dearborn, Akshaya Rajkumar, 5, in traditional dress from India, performed "God Bless America" with the International Institute Children's Choir. JENNIFER HACK

PERVASIVE PATRIOTISM

People improvised after the Sept. 11 attacks, and soon flags appeared everywhere, made of paper, crayon, paint, sequins, beads. The displays became a community battle cry, and a mourning call, like at Ken Bruce's party store on West Vernor near Clark Park in Detroit. In late October, his chalkboard reminded patrons of his ethnic heritage and compassion for the 9/11 victims. That section of Detroit had been for decades a predominantly Spanish-speaking neighborhood. The party store was unique to metro Detroit; other areas called them convenience stories. **KENT PHILLIPS**

The Riverside Ford dealership on East Jefferson near downtown Detroit added the flag to its window display in October. Owner Nate Conyers was one of the city's major black businessmen. **MANDI WRIGHT**

Six weeks after the attack, a large gathering in Windsor displayed U.S. and Canadian flags in a show of solidarity. Heightened security caused long delays at the bridge and tunnel crossings as border police scrutinized people entering the United States. **HUGH GRANNUM**

Halloween 2001 challenged celebrants to wear their patriotism in costume and cosmetics. Ninfa Negrete of Northville, a nurse, chose her face paint to cheer her patients. "It was good for everybody to see," she said. **ERIC SEALS**

A resale shop on Cass. The street in 2001 was showing some verve after years as the avenue of Detroit's destitute. Poverty and patriotism. **MANDI WRIGHT**

The Village Theatre in Ann Arbor painted its flag and message for patrons. "United We Stand" rivaled "God Bless America" as the common printed rallying cry. **KENT PHILLIPS**

Raja Rani, a restaurant with Indian fare in Ann Arbor, added a flag to its display. People from India were the leading immigrant group to southeastern Michigan in the early 1980s. **KENT PHILLIPS**

Three days after 9/11: Vincent Soulsby stood at his makeshift collection station in the parking lot of a Meijer grocery and general goods store in Roseville. He set it up for donated supplies for victims' families and rescuers in New York. J. KYLE KEENER

Six days after 9/11: Helen Longino of Detroit cheered at a flag rally in Pontiac. Rallies were held to help us share our spirit, outrage and grief. We were amazed at how quickly the country united. JENNIFER HACK

Two days after 9/11: Ann Bocci of Bloomfield Hills held two flags to purchase at American Flag and Banner in Clawson. Flags sold rapidly everywhere in metro Detroit. RICHARD LEE

Five weeks after 9/11: Watching flags flap into tatters was not uncommon. This flag flew at a gasoline station on McNichols just east of the Lodge Freeway. PATRICIA BECK

One month after 9/11: An older pickup in southwest Detroit displayed pride. Pickup trucks had become commonplace. The nation's best-selling vehicle in 2001 was the Ford F series pickup — 911,597 units. J. KYLE KEENER

Six weeks after 9/11: Street vendors like Tim Norquist met the need for colors or T-shirts with messages. His makeshift store was at Moross and I-94. KIRTHMON F. DOZIER

WE CHERISHED OUR FREEDOM

Darius Fowlkes, 12, and sister Taylor Fowlkes, 7, stood with mother Darlene Marion at their Pontiac home. Like so many families, they discovered after 9/11 the importance and the cost of freedom. "America is a great country and it's ours," Marion told her children. "We don't want anyone to take our freedom away."

J. KYLE KEENER

FLAG IN DEEP, DEEP CENTER

Numerous billboards were decorated with flags. This one stood at Trumbull just east of Kaline Drive near the center field bleacher entrance to Tiger Stadium. For more than a century, this spot served as our fortress of all that was American. But the last Tigers game was played there in 1999. And in the years that immediately followed, the stadium's future became like a well-worn ball that was batted about. By late 2001, it appeared that a Northville developer with a $170-million plan had a shot at converting the ballpark into shops, a sports club and 180 loft apartments. The field would remain, with 8,000 seats for Little League games, but the north wall along Kaline Drive would be demolished for the sports club. **PATRICIA BECK**

Dozens of flags were made by jamming colored plastic drinking cups into chain-link fences, like this one at a home in Troy. Some artists painted the ends of white styrofoam cups to get the flag effect before sticking then into fences. **RICHARD LEE**

Flags straddled the napkin holder at Janet's Lunch in Grosse Pointe Park, a cafe with a 1950s ambiance in the early 21st Century. **NANCY ANDREWS**

Ironworker Nathan Tramontana of Redford displayed his colors on his protective helmet while working in early December on Ford Field, the Lions new football stadium. **MANDI WRIGHT**

T-shirts were the most common flags-as-clothing. This person wore a top of sequins forming stars and stripes to a music video filming for singer Kid Rock. **KIRTHMON F. DOZIER**

You entered Lafayette Coney downtown for a takeout lunch of two hot dogs, no onions, please. Ahmed Noman, left, or Ali Alhalmi would relay that order to the cook: "TWO-TO-GO, WITHOUT!" It was a familiar Detroit cry, seasoned with their old-country accents. Noman was a 22-year Lafayette vet in 2001; Alhalmi, 25. **MANDI WRIGHT**

University of Michigan football players Chris Perry, left, Jonathan Goodwin and Andy Mignery stand on the sidelines during the national anthem before kickoff in October in a game against Purdue.
JULIAN H. GONZALEZ

OH, SAY CAN YOU SEE

We raised our flags and opened our wallets to aid the thousands of Sept. 11 victims. Rallies like the one shown here were organized throughout the region. At Freedom Hill in Sterling Heights, haunting images of the flag helped raise funds for the Red Cross. This photograph was taken as the national anthem played. We were not sure where this new war would take us, or how we would win. But we clung to the proud belief that we would not fail. **PAUL GONZALEZ VIDELA**

OUR FUTURE MARCHES ON *(next page)*

We wanted what these children had in 2001: to walk in sunshine, smiling broadly, full of hope. Most of us craved a life of peace for our children and knew justice, uniformly practiced, would lead to just that. These children were returning to their second-grade classroom at Genesis Elementary School after morning mass at St. Raymond Catholic Church in northeast Detroit days after Sept. 11. From left are Lamar Thomas, Carmisha Irby, Andre Pruitt, Justice Caldwell, Tiona Turner, Hydeia Woods and DeShawna Darden. They were all 7 but DeShawna, who was 6. In church they prayed. They fidgeted in the pews. When mass had ended, each was given a small American flag and then led in song: "America the Beautiful." . . . And crown thy good with brotherhood . . . In the second grade, our children believed in that notion. And most of us in 2001, in the year Detroit turned 300, tried to live up to it, too. **J. KYLE KEENER**

A runner crossing Kercheval in Detroit's Indian Village area during the annual Free Press marathon held in October hefted flags for much of the 26-mile course. **NANCY ANDREWS**

Every day, Detroit Free Press photographers make pictures they hope merit publication not only for the art of the images, but also for the truthfulness of each depiction.

The requirement that the image be fair and accurate marks a major difference between photojournalism and art photography.

Newsprint becomes the gallery wall for Free Press photographers. It is uncommon to see newspaper pictures printed as elegantly as you find them in "Time Frames." Newspaper images have 170 dots of information per inch; in "Time Frames," the number jumps to 350.

Colonies of artists are a collection of diverse souls. A newspaper photography department is, too. At the Free Press, our colony thrives on a collective energy fueled by individual creativity.

Journalism, too, is more craft than science. Our charge daily is to bring Free Press readers details of the events that impact their lives. And we work to make those events compelling and interesting through words, headlines, graphics and photography.

The entire Free Press staff, thus, has influenced "Time Frames." On the following pages we offer the biographies of the "Time Frames" staff. After reading them, we hope you'll have a more complete picture of that collection of diverse souls.

— *Nancy Andrews*

NANCY ANDREWS

The 27 members of the photography staff call Nancy Andrews the Vortex. That's because of her insatiable appetite to talk and live photography. It's also her nickname on her department's team bowling shirt.

Andrews, 38, was named Free Press director of photography in July 2000. She was previously a staff photographer at the Washington Post for 10 years. In 1999, Andrews was the White House News Photographers' Association Photographer of the Year. She was named the Newspaper Photographer of the Year for 1998 by the National Press Photographers Association and the University of Missouri's 55th Annual Pictures of the Year. She has amassed more than 100 awards from World Press Photo, United Nations and state and national press associations.

The Virginia Museum of Fine Arts awarded her an artist fellowship in 1994. She has been a frequent judge and lecturer throughout the country.

Her books include "Partial View: An Alzheimer's Journal" (Southern Methodist University Press, 1998), and "Family: A Portrait of Gay and Lesbian America" (HarperCollins Publishers, 1994).

She has had solo exhibitions at the Corcoran Gallery of Art in Washington, D.C., the Rochester Institute of Technology in New York, the Newseum in Arlington, Va., and the Bayly Art Museum in Charlottesville, Va. Her work is in the permanent collections at the Corcoran and the Bayly.

Andrews' first newspaper job was at the Cavalier Daily in Charlottesville, Va., where she worked from 1985-86 as managing editor. She then worked from 1986 to 1990 at the Free Lance-Star in Fredericksburg, Va., as a staff photographer.

Andrews graduated from the University of Virginia in 1986 with a bachelor's degree in economics.

WILLIAM ARCHIE

William Archie loves to travel and has visited 42 countries on six continents. As a Free Press photographer, he's also covered stories in Mexico, Honduras, Spain, Hong Kong, Borneo and India. Born in 1949 in Detroit, Archie spent three years working as a freelance photographer in Detroit's J. Edward Bailey Studios in the late 1970s. The Free Press hired him as a staff photographer in 1979. Two years later, he earned a bachelor of arts degree in fine arts from Wayne State University in Detroit.

Archie has won awards from the Associated Press and the Michigan Press Photographers Association. In 1989, he worked on "In Search of the Midwest," a weeklong series focusing on life in middle America.

PATRICIA BECK

A Free Press photographer for 25 years, Patricia Beck also has her work in the contemporary photography collection at the Bibliotheque Nationale in Paris. In 1984-85, Beck was a regular guest lecturer at Parson's School of Design in Paris and has returned occasionally to speak.

Beck was born in Detroit in 1953 and graduated in 1975 with honors from Ohio University with a bachelor of science degree in journalism.

She received one of journalism's highest honors, the grand prize of the Robert F. Kennedy Award for Outstanding Coverage of the Problems of the Disadvantaged, for a 1990 series "Workers at Risk." The series was the culmination of a yearlong investigation on workplace injuries in the automotive industry.

Beck has earned numerous awards from journalism organizations, including the National Press Photographers Association, the Michigan Press Photographers Association, United Press International, the Michigan Press Association, the Society of News Design, Associated Press, Women in Communications, the Detroit Press Club and Ohio University. Several civic organizations have honored her.

She has participated in numerous group exhibitions at local galleries and other venues.

Beck also taught a graduate photography course at the University of Michigan in Ann Arbor in 1996.

Among Beck's more significant work are photostories on six residents of one of Michigan's first group homes for developmentally disabled people; needy foreign children helped by a nonprofit group that secures donated medical and surgical care; one person's experience with dying and hospice care; the journey of a Michigan girl's donated organs; a single dad's adoption; life and factory work in Mexico; the America's Cup in Australia, and Miss Ratliff's first year as a Detroit public school teacher.

GINA BRINTLEY

Born in 1959 in Detroit, Gina Brintley joined the Free Press in October 1978 as an editorial assistant, believing that the job was a temporary one. She had applied for a month-long vacancy at the urging of her sister, a Free Press employee. More than two decades later, both sisters were still at the Free Press. Brintley has worked as a Free Press copy assistant and a general clerk, and in 1997 became its photography clerk. She attended Wayne State University.

SHERITA WYCHE BRYANT

Sherita Wyche Bryant, 28, is a Free Press copy editor. She grew up in Troy and and graduated from Troy Athens High School and Michigan State University, a place she loved for its natural beauty and serenity.

Bryant started working at the Free Press in February 1997. Before that, she worked summers as an intern for the Philadelphia Inquirer and the Chicago Tribune. She enjoys literature, history and traveling with her husband, Christopher.

NAHEED CHOUDHRY

Born in 1978 in Trenton, Naheed Choudhry started at the Free Press in April 2001 as a photography lab assistant. She has a love of art, and makes music, takes photographs, dances, sings and paints.

She had previously worked as a reporter and photographer at the Armada Times and as a reporter for the Daily Tribune in Royal Oak. In 2001, she earned a bachelor of arts degree in journalism from Wayne State University.

JOHN COLLIER

John Collier retired from the Free Press in 2001 after a 32-year career as a staff photographer. Born in 1943 in Abilene, Texas, Collier received a bachelor of arts degree in journalism and a master's degree in fine, performing and communications arts from Wayne State University in Detroit.

Collier received a National Endowment for the Humanities Journalism Fellowship at the University of Michigan in 1976 and has exhibited his work at the Detroit Institute of Arts. His work graced the cover of movie actress Lauren Bacall's autobiography, "By Myself." He was published in the last weekly issue of Life magazine and in the first issue of People magazine. His poetry and photographs have appeared in the Ontario Review literary magazine. His films have been screened at various film festivals, including the Ann Arbor Film Festival. He has received numerous awards, including the Michigan Press Photographer of the Year in 1973, '74 and '75.

TODD CROSS

Todd Cross became a picture editor in the Free Press features department in November 2001. Photography had taken him great distances. After graduating from Ohio University in 1992, he took a job in Egypt as a staff photographer for IBA Publications.

Cross moved to Hamburg, Germany, in 1995 and began working for the Transglobe Picture Agency. A few months later, he accepted a job at the Washington Post, leaving that newspaper in 2001 as a picture editor.

KIRTHMON F. DOZIER

Kirthmon F. Dozier was 12 when he borrowed a Mamiya 2.25 camera to earn a Boy Scout merit badge in photography.

Born in 1958 in Ft. Bragg, N.C., Dozier earned a bachelor of arts degree in communications from Washington State University.

In 1995, the Free Press hired him as a staff photographer. Prior to that, he had spent two years at New York Newsday, six years at the Detroit News and five at the Bellingham Herald in Washington.

His work was part of photography books covering the Detroit Pistons basketball team's championships in 1989 and 1990. He also covered the conflict in Somalia, the release of Nelson Mandela from prison in South Africa, the Summer Olympics in Barcelona, Spain, and U.S. peacekeeping troops in Kosovo.

PETER GAVRILOVICH

Peter Gavrilovich, 53, began a Free Press career when journalists wore eyeshades, used upright telephones and yelled COPY! when they wanted a sharpened pencil or cup of coffee. That was in 1966.

Gavrilovich's first job was as a copy boy, the old-school name for a newsroom clerk. In 1967, he spent one year as a news aide at the Washington Post and returned to the Free Press in 1968. He served from 1969 to 1971 in the U.S. Army at posts in Georgia and South Korea. Returning to the Free Press, Gavrilovich was a reporter on the Action Line column, a feature writer, a general assignment reporter, an assistant city editor, outstate Michigan correspondent, Macomb County editor, city life columnist and senior reporter and, since 1993, the deputy nation/world editor.

He was president of his senior class at Denby High School, January 1966. He attended Wayne State University and the American University in Washington, D.C.

An east sider for more than 50 years, he is co-editor of the Detroit Almanac, published by the Free Press in 2000.

In 2001, Gavrilovich coordinated the newspaper's coverage of Detroit's tricentennial celebration. From 1984 to 1988 he was a journalism instructor at the University of Detroit. He is a frequent speaker on Detroit history.

DAVID P. GILKEY

Born in 1966 in Portland, Ore., David P. Gilkey spent the final three months of Detroit's 300th year covering the war in Afghanistan. It was, he said, the hardest assignment he had ever had. "Nothing was normal," he said. "There was no water, no food you could eat that wouldn't make you sick, no electricity." When asked whether he would go back, Gilkey said without pause, "Definitely."

Gilkey studied journalism at Oregon State University and then worked at the Boulder Daily Camera in Colorado, handling local assignments for the newspaper and overseas assignments for Knight Ridder, then that paper's parent company and the parent company of the Free Press. He joined the Free Press in 1995.

Gilkey photographed the fall of apartheid in South Africa, famine in Somalia, tribal warfare in Rwanda and the conflict in Kosovo. He has earned numerous awards from the National Press Photographers Association, the Michigan Press Photographers Association, World Press Photo and the Associated Press.

JULIAN H. GONZALEZ

Julian H. Gonzalez has covered Detroit sports as a Free Press photographer since 1990. He has covered the Olympics, the Pan Am Games, auto races, and basketball, hockey, golf and track championships.

Born in 1954 in Topeka, Kan., Gonzalez was a U.S. Marine from May 1972 until October 1975. He earned a bachelor of science degree in photojournalism sequence from the University of Kansas in 1983.

Before joining the Free Press, Gonzalez spent nearly two years as a photographer for the Detroit News. He had also worked as a photographer for Gannett Rochester Newspapers in Rochester, N.Y., the Lafayette Journal & Courier in Lafayette, Ind., and the Lawrence Journal World in Lawrence, Kan. He has received numerous awards from press photographers associations in Kansas, Indiana, New York and Michigan. He was also honored by the National Press Photographers Association in association with the University of Missouri's Pictures of the Year. His photos have appeared in Time, Newsweek and Sports Illustrated magazines. He was a contributor to an exhibit on women in sports at the Smithsonian Institution in Washington, D.C.

HUGH GRANNUM

Born in 1940 in Brooklyn, N.Y., Hugh Grannum joined the Free Press in 1970 as a staff photographer. He is a graduate of Brooklyn College.

His work has been recognized by the Michigan Press Photographers Association, and the Scarab Club honored him in 1972 for an exhibition called "Detroit Dancing."

In 1981, Children's Hospital of Michigan gave him a special award for a photo series on the emergency room and burn unit. He received an individual artist's grant from the Michigan Council of the Arts in 1983 and an Arts Foundation of Michigan Creative Artists Grant in 1985.

He taught photography at Wayne County Community College, the Center for Creative Studies, Oakland Community College and Wayne State University.

Grannum has had one-man exhibitions at the Studio Museum of Harlem, N.Y.; Arts Extended Gallery; Your Heritage House (Children Museum), and the Children's Hospital of Michigan. He contributed pieces to the Black Photographers Annual, a touring exhibit seen in the United States, Europe and Russia from 1973 to 1975; the National Conference of Artists in Dakar, Senegal, in 1985, and the "Spirit of Dance" tour of 1986-1990.

His work is part of the permanent collection of the Del Pryor Gallery in Detroit. His books include "Collection of African American Art," about the collection of Detroit physician Dr. Walter O. Evans. His works are in the collection at the Detroit Institute of Arts.

MAURICIO GUTIERREZ

Mauricio Gutierrez, a native of Monterrey, Mexico, worked in Mexico and Spain before joining the Free Press in 2000. He is deputy design director/features at the Free Press.

Gutierrez, 31, graduated from the Instituto Tecnologico y de Estudios Superiores de Monterrey in 1992 with a degree in mass media.

Before joining the Free Press, Gutierrez was a designer at the Orange County Register, Santa Ana, Calif., from 1998-2000; senior graphic designer from 1989-1994, and then art director in 1998 at El Norte, Monterrey, Mexico. From 1994-98, Gutierrez was a designer and art director at two studios in Barcelona, Spain. He is the recipient of numerous design awards from professional organizations in California and Spain and counts eight awards of excellence from the Society for News Design.

JENNIFER HACK

Born in 1980 in Kansas City, Mo., Jennifer Hack came to the Free Press in the fall of 2001 as a Knight Ridder scholar from the University of Missouri.

She completed a 4-month photography internship at the Free Press.

ED HAUN

Ed Haun is the Free Press employee with the most seniority. Born in 1935 in Detroit, he began his tenure at the Free Press in 1957 as a photographer's assistant working on color projects.

Haun became a Free Press staff photographer in 1958. A year later, he covered the '59ers homesteading to Alaska. He photographed the Essex wire strike in Hillsdale, and the 1966 civil disturbance and 1967 riot in Detroit. He was part of the Free Press staff that won the Pulitzer Prize for coverage of that riot.

He also photographed the Algiers Motel incident in 1967 and the sinking of a British freighter, the Montrose, on the Detroit River in 1962. The Michigan Press Photographers Association, the Inland Daily Press Association and the Associated Press have honored Haun for his work. He has covered various sporting events, including the 1968 World Series.

In 1975, he moved from the streets to the newspaper's darkroom, handling in-house color processing. Haun now maintains the photography department's machinery.

AZLAN IBRAHIM

Azlan Ibrahim was born in Singapore and educated in an anglophone prep school in Malaysia, where he learned to love cricket, tea and the BBC World Service. Ibrahim, 33, graduated from Western Michigan University with a bachelor of arts degree in English and political science in 1992 and a master of fine arts degree in 1995.

He began his journalism career in 1988 in Malaysia at the New Straits Times as a general assignment reporter.

Ibrahim became an editor at the Kalamazoo Gazette in 1997. He joined the Free Press in 2000 as a copy editor, and is also working as an assistant nation/world editor.

He plays defense on the Free Press soccer team and does yoga, tai chi and the tango in his spare time.

ANDREW JOHNSTON

Born in 1964 in Indianapolis, Ind., Andrew Johnston joined the Free Press in July 1998 as a features picture editor and was named picture editor for news in 2000.

He is an avid fisherman, devoting much of his free time to the Detroit River and Lake St. Clair.

Before coming to the Free Press, Johnston had spent 15 months as a freelance photojournalist and eight years as a staff photographer at the Journal Gazette in Fort Wayne, Ind.

He was a staff photographer for Outdoor Indiana magazine in Indianapolis in 1987 and 1988, and trained with a forest firefighting crew in southwest Oregon so that he could photograph the team's work.

Johnston graduated from Ball State University in 1987 with a bachelor's degree in journalism and graphics arts technology. He has received numerous awards from the Society for News Design, the Michigan Press Photographers Association and the University of Missouri's Pictures of the Year.

KAREN JOSEPH

Karen Joseph has been a Free Press copy editor since May 2001. Born in 1972 in Royal Oak, she is a 1994 graduate of Central Michigan University, where she majored in journalism and English.

Joseph began her newspaper career as a reporter at the Traverse City Record-Eagle. She joined the Ann Arbor News as a reporter in 1996 and the Riverside Press-Enterprise, Riverside, Calif., as a reporter in 1999. She worked in 2000 as a copy editor at the Los Angeles Times.

In 1999, she was awarded a first place for enterprise reporting from the Los Angeles chapter of the Society of Professional Journalists.

J. KYLE KEENER

J. Kyle Keener was named Free Press chief photographer in 2001. He has been a staff photographer with the Free Press since 1995.

Born in 1960 in Cincinnati, Ohio, he spent nine years as a staff photographer at the Philadelphia Inquirer and two years as a photographer at the Kansas City Times in Missouri.

He graduated from Central Michigan University in 1983 with a bachelor of arts degree in journalism.

Keener has covered the AIDS epidemic in Africa in 1987, the destruction of the Amazon rain forest in 1989, the end of apartheid in South Africa in 1991-92 and the aftermath of the Rwanda genocide in 1994. The National Press Photographers Association has

honored him six times as its Regional Photographer of the Year and he received numerous awards from the Michigan Press Photographers Association, the Associated Press, the Society for News Design and the University of Missouri's Pictures of the Year.

Keener taught art direction at the Poynter Institute, a St. Petersburg, Fla., school for journalists. He has also lectured widely and judged state photojournalism conferences across the country. In 2001, Keener began "Keenervision," an occasional photo column that illustrates a specific human aspect. He said he believed that images that captured simple human expressions and values forged connections between people.

RICHARD LEE

Born in 1944 in Singapore, Richard Lee joined the Free Press as a staff photographer in 1972.

He completed high school in Singapore and continued his education in London and in Ann Arbor at the University of Michigan. He discovered his love of photojournalism at U-M, capturing images of Vietnam War protests.

Lee taught photography to students in adult education classes in Troy. His awards include recognition from the National Press Photographers Association.

ROSE ANN McKEAN

Rose Ann McKean runs at least 3 miles daily before coming to work, where she is a laboratory technician in the Free Press photography department. In 1999, she ran in the Free Press marathon.

Born in 1962 in Detroit, McKean is also a student at the University of Michigan in Dearborn.

Her first Free Press job was in 1981 as a customer service clerk in the circulation department. She later worked as a clerk and office coordinator in the purchasing department.

McKean has worked on other Free Press books, including "The Corner" and "Corner to Copa," about the Detroit Tigers baseball team and its stadiums, and the Detroit Almanac, a chronicle of the city's first 300 years.

KENT PHILLIPS

Photographers aren't all about focus, film and frames. Kent Phillips spent two summers as a street juggler at Busch Gardens in Williamsburg, Va., and once juggled an axe, bowling ball and rubber chicken on national cable television. He spent five years as a volunteer firefighter.

Born in 1965 in Silver Spring, Md., Phillips joined the Free Press in January 2000 as a staff photographer. He had worked for four years at the Commercial Appeal in Memphis, Tenn., and for seven years at the Herald-Times in Bloomington, Ind. He freelanced extensively while living in Memphis.

Phillips earned a bachelor's degree with a major in journalism and a minor in fine arts in 1990 from Indiana University. He served as photo adviser for the Eastern Echo, Eastern Michigan University's student newspaper, in 2001-02.

Phillips has won numerous awards from the Society of News Design, the National Press Photographers Association and the University of Missouri's Pictures of the Year.

CRAIG PORTER

Born an identical twin in 1952 in Fort Lee,

Va., Craig Porter came to the Free Press in 1975 as a summer photography intern from Michigan State University and joined the staff full-time in 1976.

Since then, he has worked as a photographer, features photo editor, night photo editor, assistant director of photography and technology, and deputy director of photography.

Stories have taken him across Michigan and the United States and to Iraq in the aftermath of Operation Desert Storm. He has received numerous state and local photography awards.

MARY SCHROEDER

Mary Schroeder had never been to a professional baseball or hockey game when she began shooting sports soon after she was hired as a Free Press photographer in 1979.

Born in 1957 in Manitowoc, Wis., Schroeder planned to work four months, then pursue a master's degree at Ohio University, until she was hired full-time a month into her internship.

In 1983, she was assigned to cover sports full-time. Her image of Detroit Tiger Kirk Gibson roaring after he hit a home run in the final game of the 1984 World Series against the San Diego Padres became one of the city's most recognizable photographs. Her photographs are displayed in the Baseball Hall of Fame in Cooperstown, N.Y., and in the Football Hall of Fame in Canton, Ohio.

In the early 1990s, she started handling assignments throughout the newspaper and steering photo coverage.

Schroeder is an avid sailor and has won numerous regattas. She is the main sail trimmer on Allegiance, a Frers 50 owned by Don and Helen Holstein of St. Clair Shores.

ERIC SEALS

Born in 1969 in Detroit, Eric Seals knew from the time he was in 10th grade that he wanted to be a photojournalist. Seals was a one-year photo intern at the Free Press in 1993-94 and returned to the paper in January 1999 as a staff photographer.

Seals worked at the State newspaper in Columbia, S.C., from 1995 to 1999. He was named the South Carolina Photographer of the Year in 1995 by that state's News Photographers Association. He covered both presidential campaigns of former President Bill Clinton; the Northridge earthquake in California in 1993; wildfires in Florida in 1997; the story of Susan Smith, who drowned her two young sons in a car in Union, S.C.; the entrance of the first women at the Citadel, formerly an all-male military school in Charleston, S.C.; the college basketball tournament that made Michigan State University national champs, and the inauguration of President George W. Bush.

Seals earned a bachelor's degree in journalism from the University of Missouri in 1993. He was a member of the faculty at the Truth with a Camera Workshop in Portsmouth, Va., in 1996 and 1997.

CHIP SOMODEVILLA

While a photojournalism instructor at Purdue University's Fort Wayne campus in Indiana, Chip Somodevilla urged that journalists should make their range of experiences broad.

Somodevilla did. He chalked baseball diamonds, cleaned swimming pools, installed carpet and floor tiles, sold shoes to athletes and sold bathing suits to women. He was also an altar server for his father, an Episcopalian priest. "As a journalist, you've got to know a little something about